ROUTLEDGE LIBRARY EDITIONS:
BUSINESS AND ECONOMICS IN ASIA

Volume 11

ECONOMIC MAN IN SHA TIN

ECONOMIC MAN IN SHA TIN
Vegetable Gardeners in a Hong Kong Valley

GÖRAN AIJMER

Routledge
Taylor & Francis Group

LONDON AND NEW YORK

First published in 1980 by Curzon Press Ltd

This edition first published in 2019
by Routledge
2 Park Square, Milton Park, Abingdon, Oxon OX14 4RN

and by Routledge
52 Vanderbilt Avenue, New York, NY 10017

Routledge is an imprint of the Taylor & Francis Group, an informa business

© 1979 Göran Aijmer

British Library Cataloguing in Publication Data
A catalogue record for this book is available from the British Library

ISBN: 978-1-138-48274-6 (Set)
ISBN: 978-0-429-42825-8 (Set) (ebk)
ISBN: 978-1-138-36800-2 (Volume 11) (hbk)
ISBN: 978-0-429-42947-7 (Volume 11) (ebk)

Publisher's Note
The publisher has gone to great lengths to ensure the quality of this reprint but points out that some imperfections in the original copies may be apparent.

Disclaimer
The publisher has made every effort to trace copyright holders and would welcome correspondence from those they have been unable to trace.

SCANDINAVIAN INSTITUTE OF ASIAN STUDIES
MONOGRAPH SERIES   NO 43

Economic Man in Sha Tin

Vegetable Gardeners in a Hong Kong Valley

Göran Aijmer

Curzon Press

Scandinavian Institute of Asian Studies
Kejsergade 2, DK-1155 Copenhagen K

First published 1980
Curzon Press Ltd: London and Malmö

© Göran Aijmer 1979

ISBN 0 7007 0135 4
ISSN 0069 1712

This book was printed with the aid of a
grant from the Swedish Statens Humanistisk-
Samhällsvetenskapliga Forskningsråd.

Printed in Great Britain by
Biddles Ltd, Guildford, Surrey

CONTENTS

MAPS

ILLUSTRATIONS

PREFACE

The present work is a contribution to the descriptive
sociology of Chinese society. It deals with socio-
economic processes on the urban fringe, it aims at
bringing about knowledge of the Sha Tin valley in the
New Territories of Hong Kong, situated close to the
great conurbation of Hongkong-Kowloon, and it discusses
the Sha Tin findings in a comparison with other data
from China. Only part of what I learnt in Sha Tin is
presented here, and a sequel volume to the present one
is planned to deal more with social relationships and
processes of interaction among immigrant vegetable
farmers of that New Territories valley.

This work is an anthropologist's account of how
refugee immigrants from China make a living as market
gardeners in a valley of the rural areas of the British
Crown Colony of Hong Kong. It is based on field work
in the late 1960s (the 'ethnographical present' of the
book) and using an actor-oriented perspective it
examines various aspects of economic life; the discussion
concerns both individual economic adaptations and such
socio-economic structures as unfold to the gardeners in
that adaptation. The argument of the work will start
with descriptions and analyses of what people actually
do as market gardeners in an attempt to explore their
doings in terms of their own understanding of the
universe of Hong Kong. This inquiry leads to a wider
consideration of agricultural change. Finally the
Hong Kong observations are discussed and systematized
into a comparative Chinese framework.

The account which follows here is a description and
discussion of what might be called a transitional period
in the history of the New Territories. The conditions
which are reported on here have changed profoundly.
The Sha Tin valley sees today a new city emerge. At a
very brief visit to the area in late 1978 I saw that
some parts of the valley in which I worked a decade
earlier had not yet been touched directly by the
enormous development which takes place. The villages
now have many new houses, commercial and residential
buildings, which reflect a new prosperity of the Sha Tin
natives, probably derived from land transactions in
connection with the urbanization of the area. Sha Tin
is rapidly becoming 'modern' in the sense that the
valley becomes increasingly integrated in the industrial
complex of the Colony. My observations from the late
1960s may then also have some documentary value.

This book is a result of many circumstances. In the first place it reflects the fact that it was possible to carry out some sort of field work in the New Territories of Hong Kong in the last few years of the 1960s, despite the inflamed situation caused by the Chinese 'Cultural Revolution' and its overspill into the British Crown Colony. Again it reflects that the people of the New Territories, despite their misgivings over European foreigners and Chinese political bosses, were willing to discuss the construction of their daily lives. I remain deeply indebted to all my informants in the Sha Tin valley for the generosity and concern with which they provided me with information.

Other felicitous circumstances for this work have been the sponsorships of the Swedish Research Council for the Humanities which contributed to the founding of the two main fieldwork periods in Hong Kong, and of the University of Stockholm and the Carl-Bertel Nathorst Foundation which made possible a period of writing and contemplation in the United States. I wish to express my gratitude to the Harvard-Yenching Institute, Harvard University, for their receiving me and for their hospitality. It was during my visit there in 1970 that I drafted the best part of this book.

The sometimes strained circumstances of fieldwork can be eased by help, advice, and encouragement. My residence in Hong Kong was made rich and profitable by many people. Especially, I wish to thank John Cheong, John Chow, Anthony and Victoria Dicks, James Hayes, C.T. Leung, Samuel Leung, Howard Nelson, Sten and Lai-yin Stenquist, and a great number of staff members of the New Territories administration.

Many others have contributed to the work. With special gratitude I wish to mention Karin Aijmer, the late Maurice Freedman, Ulf Hannerz, Ezra Vogel, and Eugene Wu.

I have read papers on topics dealt with in this book at seminars at the University of Hong Kong, and the University of Stockholm. I remain thankful for these opportunities. Finally, I wish to express my appreciation of editorial help from Lois Egerod.

Gothenburg, 1979   Göran Aijmer

I. THE SHA TIN VALLEY: SOME INTRODUCTORY REMARKS

Beyond the high mountains which separate the bustling
city of Kowloon from the mainland part of the British
Crown Colony of Hong Kong, known as the New Territories,
lies the spectacular valley of Sha Tin – Sandy Fields.
This essay is a discussion of some aspects of rural
economic activities in this valley on the basis of my
observations in the years 1967-9.

My first experience of Sha Tin was in 1964 when as a
newcomer to the New Territories I was looking around for
a suitable village for field-work. Later, during field-
work for ten months with three Hakka settlements in the
Ma On Shan area, I often had an opportunity of coming
down to the market-town in the valley. I caught some
further glimpses of the valley during a brief visit to
Hong Kong in 1966. When I renewed the contact with
Sha Tin in June 1967 with the purpose of initiating
field-work which was to last for nearly thirteen months
(June 1967-February 1968, June-September 1969) on rural
immigrants in the New Territories, I was thus not
entirely without knowledge of the Sha Tin valley; this
certainly influenced my choice of this particular area
for my new investigations. Although I had travelled to
most corners of the New Territories, the impressions I
had formed of other possible areas for the field-work I
had in mind were inadequate. If my knowledge of Sha Tin
was a little less so, it was still far from sufficient.
It may be that if I had then realized the difficulties
I was heading for, this study might not have come about
at all.

Part of the attraction of conducting an investigation
of social life in the Sha Tin valley was that this area
is intended for a large-scale development into a
satellite city of the great conurbation of Hongkong[1]-
Kowloon. The mountainous character of the colony has
contributed to an increasing demand for new industrial
and residential land outside the Victoria Harbour area,
where, on the whole, new building sites can be obtained
only by way of very costly reclamation. In the New
Territories, Tsuen Wan has already been turned into an
industrial city and plans are being entertained to
carry out a similar development of Castle Peak and
Sha Tin. It is intended that half a million people or
more will inhabit Sha Tin.[2]

The Sha Tin valley is close to Kowloon and sheltered
from the metropolis by a high range of mountains which
has hitherto stopped urban expansion in this direction.

1

Communication with the city is made possible over the
Sha Tin pass (the traditional road) by way of a narrow
and winding road, and since 1967 by means of a new road
leading through a tunnel, thus affording rapid passage
to upper Kowloon. Also, the Kowloon-Canton Railway
maintains a train service. A traveller from Sha Tin
will find convenient stops in Yau Ma Tei and Tsim Sha
Tsui. Trains leave in both directions about once every
forty minutes from the early morning until late in the
evening. A bus service operates more frequently and
avails itself of both roads. Relatively good transportation services have made Sha Tin attractive as a
residential area for people working in Kowloon, and an
unknown number of people commute daily from the valley
to their factories and offices.

The Sha Tin valley opens up towards the southern
inlet of Tolo Harbour known as Tide Cove. It is an area
of approximately 2,000 acres of low and relatively low
land surrounded by very steep mountains, some of which
reach a height of 1,750 feet. From Tide Cove the valley
extends in a southwesterly direction for nearly two
miles. By long usage Sha Tin is an agricultural area
dotted with many small villages. However, present-day
development has left large tracts of arable land
abandoned. The villages have seen the arrival of small-
scale cottage industries and there are even a few
industrial plants of considerable size in the valley.
Before the arrival of the British in 1899 Sha Tin was a
remote part of Xinan District (nowadays Baoan), a part
of a rugged piece of coastal land frequently visited by
pirates. It was a troublesome area for the officials
and military both in the district capital and in the
small local governmental offices and garrisons. In Sha
Tin there were no grand-scale lineages inhabiting the
villages. Each village harboured smaller kinship groups.
Some places are exclusively inhabited by one single
lineage, and a few lineages have branches in several
villages. For instance, related people of the surname
Wei are to be found in both Tai Wai and Tin Sam, big
multi-surname villages, as well as in Sheung Keng Hau
which is inhabited exclusively by Wei. A great number
of people in the valley speak Hakka but they live close
to Cantonese speakers and the two groups are often
intermingled. Cantonese is *lingua franca* in the area.

Several monographs and many articles on the New
Territories have appeared in recent years and the area
is in no way a white spot on the ethnographic map.
Plenty of background material is to be found in print.[3]
There is no need to provide this essay with another

introduction to the New Territories. However, it may
be pointed out that much recent interest has been
devoted to the 'lineage landscape' of the area, an
obvious inheritance from the pioneering efforts of
Maurice Freedman.[4] My own interests have diverged from
this tradition and my work has concerned people outside
the structural order. A study of social flux is, of
course, of particular interest in the present-day
situation, and the relevance of such a study is not
confined to the contemporary scene. I believe that some
of my findings provide clues for a historically focused
anthropology aiming at the reconstruction of traditional
forms of rural society in Southeastern China. What can
be seen and studied in the New Territories today are
tokens of activities which have been in existence for
centuries in a country plagued by almost constant social
upheaval.

Besides the native population there exists in the New
Territories today a great number of immigrants,
arrivals from China, who left their native villages and
towns, mostly after the establishment of the People's
Republic in 1949. Their presence in Sha Tin is
numerically as strong as it is in most parts of the New
Territories. The appearance of such foreigners on the
social scene is one of the more dramatic features of
the area; not that the intrusion of outsiders was a
novelty, but because of their number they make up a
majority of the population in most places, with the
exception of the inaccessible mountain areas with their
sparse settlements. In Sha Tin only about 4,000 people
out of a population of perhaps 30,000 are native
villagers.

What initially attracted my interest was a number of
problems connected with the presence of outsiders in a
'traditionalist' society characteristically based on
the village and on lineage organization. By this I do
not mean to imply that the New Territories form a
repository for a traditional type of Southeastern
Chinese society. The New Territories have been exposed
enormously to the forces of change although the course
of history, since the British occupation in 1899, has
been very different here from what went on in China.
Still it may be said that in many respects the village
communities look towards traditional ideals of what
life should be like. The questions I raised were
simple and straightforward. Why do people come to Sha
Tin? How do they get there? How do they find a livelihood? I took an interest in issues such as the
relations between the outsiders and the natives and

Sketch Map of the B.C.C. of Hongkong

the accommodation of the indigenous population to the new situation that a great number of immigrants now live in the area. And, of course, I was interested in the relations between the outsiders themselves. This essay is an attempt to furnish some answers to these questions within the sphere of economic life.

The general aim of this study is, then, to contribute to the descriptive sociology of Chinese society. From an actor-oriented perspective I will try to account for how refugee immigrants from China make a living as market gardeners in a valley of the New Territories. I will examine various aspects of economic life. The discussion concerns both individual economic strategies and such socio-economic structures as are revealed to the gardeners in their dealings with the world.

Writing about economic life I argue as a social anthropologist. I have but a limited interest in statistics, and my experience in the field has taught me to distrust figures of averages and distributions, and other computations of hard facts. I leave such procedures to rural economists and others trained in the tradition of 'mass observation'. The collector of hard facts, interested in measuring the reality, will no doubt find that what I have to say on household finances, for instance, is cursory, and he will judge the data I present on horticulture as flimsy and hedged about with warnings of inadequacy. He may well wonder if reporting in this form justifies even a modest publication.

My experience that straightforward economic facts are extremely difficult to get at for many reasons may seem disconcerting to some, but it does not mean that I regard field-work as inadequate because it does not uncover such facts. On the contrary I think the Sha Tin effort was fairly successful in that, despite the enormous difficulties of working with a very heterogeneous lot of people in a politically heated atmosphere, it was possible to describe and analyse a great many economic activities. There is often a lack of detail (which I maintain should be treated as a sociological fact) and there are many round estimates. There are many blanks in the picture. I present here such insights as I have and I have not tried to patch up what I could not learn in the field. Still, I believe that my picture of farming life in Sha Tin is reasonably adequate and, I hope, of interest to students of various aspects of rural change, rural-urban relations, and of Chinese ethnography. In a sequel volume I will deal with social and political features of the farming community of Sha Tin.

Thus, what I have to say may be sketchy. The field-
work proved quite difficult and to obtain information
was a matter of unusual intricacy. There was an unfore-
seeable timing of my presence in Sha Tin in 1967-8 with
the outbreak of fierce political activity in Hong Kong,
a kind of overspill from the Cultural Revolution in
China. When I took up work in Sha Tin, the first phase
of violent rioting in the streets of the city areas was
more or less over, but terror bombing had replaced the
demonstrations. These activities were not confined to
the city areas but occurred in many parts of the New
Territories as well. The police forces were very alert
at the time and it was hardly surprising to find that
informants became very suspicious when a person of
foreign extraction appeared asking naive questions
about obvious things. But as time passed, and particularly on my return visit in the summer of 1969 when
things were a bit more settled, I was trusted by a
number of very helpful and understanding people.

When I started to collect field data in June 1967
my first aim was to establish an overall view of the
situation in Sha Tin. I profited from conversations
with Rural Committee members and persons in the administration, and with the help of introductions I approached
a number of village representatives and other knowledgeable persons in the villages and the market town. By
means of these talks I was able to acquire a fair, but
not very detailed knowledge of what was going on in the
villages and in the market. One main obstacle remained.
It was difficult to get in touch with outsiders, the
immigrants in the area. I had learnt from my earlier
field experience in Hong Kong that in order to approach
a person without his feeling imposed on, you needed an
introduction, or, at least, to be able to refer to a
common acquaintance. Generally such a strategy works
nicely, but when I employed chains of introductions in
Sha Tin it was only a limited success in that it brought
me in touch solely with village people. When in a
village I asked someone if he knew any immigrants in
that area, and, if so, whether he could introduce me to
any such person, it was like the closing of a door.
The general answer was "I don't know any of them," or
"I don't know anything about them except that they work
in their fields constantly and keep to themselves."
It took me some time to understand that in such answers
I had hit upon one of the most profound social features
of the valley. There exist very few links indeed
between the villagers and the immigrants. Villagers
were not consciously raising obstacles, they told the

7

truth. However, a few merchants were willing to introduce me to some of their clients who were immigrants,
and likewise I received help from the local field-staff
of the Department of Agriculture. This was my first
contact with new residents.

Soon I abandoned the strategy of introductions and
just struck up conversations with people working in the
fields, and this proved modestly successful. Often I
was given an astonished but affirmative response. It
happened also that people did not answer at all, and on
occasion I was not even given a chance to exchange
greetings and polite phrases but was met by hostility
and bad-tempered shouts. Sometimes people would fling
stones. Thus I had to rely on a limited number of helpful people and on what I could see for myself. But even
persons who were generally very forthcoming were reserved
in the pronouncements they made, especially *vis-à-vis*
their neighbours. It was all right for an immigrant
farmer to talk about himself but great reluctance was
shown as soon as the conversation drifted towards
subject matters concerning other persons, even if the
questions, as it seemed to me, were extremely innocent.

For instance, once in a heavy downpour I was squatting
beneath an umbrella together with a young man who was
always very pleasant to talk to. Suddenly we saw a man
whom I had never noticed before in the area, walking on a
path at some distance. In response to my question as to
who he was, my companion under the umbrella gave me a
blank stare and said: "Why don't you go over there and
ask him." Later I found out that the stranger was a
merchant collecting orders for seeds. Such answers were
not only due to discretion and fear of encroaching on
privacy. There was also a lingering suspicion that the
information given might be misused and could cause harm
to the community, and, furthermore, and this is most
important, the observation of self-imposed constraint in
conversation was a means of self-protection on an
unpredictable social scene.

It should be mentioned that my field-work was carried
out with the help of a Cantonese assistant. This turned
out to be of great help not only because it compensated
for my own poor knowledge of Cantonese but because it
facilitated fact-finding in a general way. Sometimes
people were more ready to talk and discuss delicate
matters in my absence although it was made quite clear
to them that the information they offered would be con-
veyed to me by my assistant. The very presence of a
European on the local scene was such a novelty that in
the relatively short periods of field work I spent in

Sha Tin the frustration caused by this could never be completely overcome, even if most people had come to realize that the foreigner was quite harmless. It was quite obvious that in many situations I profited from my nationality; coming from a country, often unknown to my informants, disassociated me from British officialdom. It should be remembered that British officials were not always held in high esteem at the time. The fact that I had travelled in China in 1966 was also in my favour.

As mentioned already, in the first stage of field-work I was interviewing people all over the valley, but gradually, the main part of my work was concentrated to the southern end around the villages of Tai Wai, Tin Sam, Kak Tin, and Keng Hau. Finally I concentrated my field-work around a cluster of immigrant huts close to the village of Ha Keng Hau, which I have called the Keng Hau neighbourhood. During the final stage of the field-work in 1969 my work was carried out almost exclusively on the people living in that settlement. I had no special rationale for selecting this particular spot for a more intense study. It only seemed suitable.

The Keng Hau neighbourhood is a rather typical cluster of dwellings. The huts are constructed of wood and tin and are situated around and in the midst of the fields of the inhabitants; they live on vegetable and flower farming which they carry out on rented land. The settlers are a heterogeneous crowd of many back-grounds.[5] But in their everyday activities in Sha Tin they look similar and do more or less the same things. This essay forms a study of their everyday life.[6]

NOTES TO CHAPTER I

1. When spelt Hongkong I mean the island city formerly known as Victoria; for the name of the Crown Colony I use the official spelling Hong Kong.
2. 'The total population upon full development is estimated to be approximately one million persons.' *Sha Tin Outline Zoning Plan*, 3.
3. See especially the introductory chapters to Baker 1968 and Potter 1968. Freedman's (1963) survey remains very valuable. Other useful papers are Anderson 1968, Hayes 1962, Potter 1969, Lo 1968, and M. Topley 1964.
4. Freedman 1958, 1966.
5. Aijmer 1973.
6. A very brief outline of what follows has appeared in Aijmer 1972.

II. ENVIRONMENTAL PREREQUISITES FOR MARKET GARDENING

It is almost trivial to point out to the reader who is somewhat acquainted with the situation in Hong Kong that the Colony is in the midst of an intense process of change, embracing most, if not all, sectors of the society. This does not only apply to the city areas on Hong Kong Island and Kowloon Peninsula where the post-war boost of industrialization has left an easily observable impact on the urban landscape and on the people who have congregated there. Also, the New Territories have been involved in this spectacular process of change and not even the most remote villages have remained unaffected by the larger society's striving for new economic achievements. Thus it is not only a question of certain minor industries[1] moving away from the costly land in the industrially and commercially developed areas along the Hong Kong harbour to find new locations in the New Territories. Social life has changed there.

A feature of change which is easily observable in the New Territories is that the cultivation of rice has been replaced by horticulture and floriculture. This replacement of one agricultural system for another has been hinted at repeatedly in the literature on the New Territories.[2] However, these remarks have hardly been accompanied by more penetrating analyses of this phase of change. Therefore, in this essay, we wish to engage in a discussion on the agricultural-economic transition which has taken place in the Sha Tin valley. It must be stressed though that we shall argue here from the point-of-view of the social anthropologist rather than from that of the rural economist. Our focus of interest will be on such social activities as may be seen as connected with economic phenomena. By and large, the perspective is actor-orientated.

It goes without saying that vegetable growing is no recent innovation, neither in Sha Tin, nor in other areas of the New Territories. Land at higher levels on the sloping mountain sides has always been used for the cultivation of certain vegetables. For instance, the Hakka-speaking mountain peasants in the relatively inaccessible mountains surrounding Sha Tin and Tide Cove still have traditional forms of vegetable cultivation. In these remote districts people used to plant vegetables on narrow terraces cut out from the hillside, together with tea bushes and indigo shrubs. Presumably the tea and the indigo were more important than the vegetables.

11

The evidence at hand indicates that vegetables were
cultivated entirely for local consumption. Today this
is definitely so in these villages.[3] It is clear also
that the cultivation of vegetables was of slight importance and was carried out on land that was not otherwise
needed. Horticulture gave only subsidiary crops. Of
more vital importance in the villages was the irrigated
rice land and to this they devoted most of their interest
and their work. The present-day situation is very
different; the Sha Tin valley is now characterized
by the superbly thriving market garden beds.

First, let us survey the ecological conditions for
vegetable growing and flower planting in the Sha Tin
valley. An authority in this field maintains that

> The main requirements of the soil are that it should
> have a loamy surface horizon which can be easily
> worked and which does not cake under repeated
> watering. The subsoil should be a clay with a high
> water-table though the hardpan residual from paddy
> cultivation is equally useful in maintaining the
> irrigation water at the correct depth.[4]

The soil of the Sha Tin valley is, to a large extent, of
an alluvial type, formed by the erosion of the surrounding
granite mountains. The result is a sandy upper layer on
top of hard granite soil, which is very favourable for
growing vegetables as well as flowers.[5] Even if it can be
said that the conditions are generally well suited for
taking up horticulture on the former rice fields, there
are still some variations in the picture. The mouth of
the Sha Tin valley is made up of low land along Tide Cove
which was exposed to heavy destruction in the years of
1954, 1962, and 1964. A long sea-wall joins the small
island of Yuen Chow Kok and the mainland to form a huge
dam. This sea-wall, which is supposed to have been
constructed in the Qing dynasty, used to shelter reclaimed
land which, apparently, was of importance for the neighbouring villages. There are other similar sea-walls
along the shore.

In 1962 there was an unusually violent typhoon. The
power of the accompanying rushing tidal waves was such
that they broke through the sea-walls and the whole of
the low-lying country was submerged. Again, a series of
five typhoons in 1964 caused new damage.[6] The whole
strip of land from Sha Tin Tau and Tsang Tai Uk to Sha
Tin Wai, and even as far as the villages Siu Lek Yuen
and Ngau Pei Sha, was under water. Every new typhoon has
caused further inundation in exposed areas. Salination

1. The farmstead of Ou Xi in the Keng Hau neighbourhood. In the foreground a field of chrysanthemum flowers.

has caused much damage in these flooded fields. It made
the continuation of rice farming impossible here, and it
has had an adverse effect at least on vegetable cultivation.

In the traditional system of farming, vegetable
growing took place on terraces carved out on the hill
sides, or on beds on higher level land. Similar terraces
are still constructed and are used either as a complement
to old arable land or as the sole asset for a new garden
enterprise. Of course, such soil is inferior to that of
old paddy fields, and costly and laborious techniques
must be used for the land to give a reasonable yield.
Gardens grown on such high-level land are common on the
slopes of the adjoining Pak Tin valley, for instance, but
they are also to be found on the lower slopes at the
bottom of the Sha Tin valley proper.

To dig out a new terrace is not an unusual enterprise
for a market gardener who wishes to expand his land.
Thus, in the Keng Hau area Weng Guiyou acquired new land
in this way during the late summer of 1969 in order to
increase his holdings. Weng set out to build the new
terrace with no technical aid but hoe and shovel. Other
more enterprising people, for example on To Fun Shan,
have had access to a bulldozer procured with the assistance of the Department of Agriculture and Fisheries of
the Hong Kong Government.

Other factors of the ecosystem which are of utmost
importance are water and temperature. Dating back a
long time Sha Tin has been an area exposed to serious
flooding and great damage was common earlier. The
reason for this was the many mountain brooks which
brought rain-water down to the valley over the steep
slopes. Thus large stretches of arable land at the
bottom of the valley, at its mouth, and in the adjoining
valley of Pak Tin, were destroyed in 1959 by the inundation that year. Compact layers of sand and mud were
spread over the fields. Another bad year was 1957.
After these events, the main river through the valley,
the Shing Mun river, has been brought under control by
way of the construction of a huge reservoir above the
Pak Tin valley. The former river has been left in a sad
state of nearly complete dryness, and now only its lower
part is flooded by the tidal waves from the sea. An
official programme of draining brought about the construction, completed in 1960, of a cement nullah with a
large capacity. It runs straight through the valley and
rapidly conducts excess water down to the lower stretch
of the Shing Mun river course and its outlet into the
sea.

The risks of inundation were further reduced after the completion of a catch-water system high up on the mountain sides, which collects the best part of the water of the streams formerly running down the steep slopes. Possibly the catch-water system has brought about a shortage of water in some areas; this is vigorously maintained by many farmers in the Sha Tin. Even these measures have not eliminated the threat of flooding, which remains. Thus a few hours of torrential monsoon rain in early August in 1969 caused an inundation of the whole of Sha Tin. People had to wade along the elevated footpaths in water more than knee-deep. The water of the Shing Mun reservoir rose until the authorities had to empty out water in order to have the overflow under control. The population of the lower areas had to be evacuated to school premises at Tai Wai. On the whole the water had receded within the next few days but the damage caused was immense.

Of course, rain-water is of great importance indirectly for the existing systems of irrigation. Originally these systems were constructed and adapted for the supply of the traditional rice cultivation. Only 6.9 per cent of the annual precipitation falls during the first three months of the year; 37.9 per cent during April, May and June, when the monsoon wind carries much rain in from the Pacific; 47.1 per cent of the rain falls in July, August, and September, which period is the peak of the typhoon season. During the last three months of the year the rainfall amounts to 8.1 per cent of the annual precipitation. The corresponding volume of rain is 148, 816, 1011, and 173 mm respectively.[7] The rainfall in Hong Kong varies due to varying altitudes in the mountainous landscape, but the conditions in Sha Tin will not be very different from those of the Royal Observatory in Kowloon.

The summer rains do not fall evenly over the twenty-four hours of the day but the largest amounts come in the early morning hours. This fact affects the working routines of the vegetable grower, who during this season will tend the manual irrigation of the gardens especially in the afternoon and evening. A prominent feature of the summer rains is that they are very violent, particularly in connection with the many thunderstorms. As mentioned above, such torrents cause flooding and destroy crops as an aftermath. This applies especially to cultivation of vegetables and flowers as not only the inundation, but also the mere force of the downpour may have devastating effects. One of the worst exposed areas of Sha Tin is the low-lying country in front of Tsang Tai Uk, a stretch

of land which is submerged in every passing rainstorm.
This circumstance, in combination with the salination
caused by the flooding from the sea, mentioned above,
accounts for the fact that only a few kinds of water
plants are cultivated there, and only to a limited
extent.

Under normal conditions the mountain streams are an
asset and most of them carry water even in the winter.
Whether this supply is sufficient during the dry season
is a matter which is disputed, as observed above. In
the Keng Hau area the water-supply is regarded as
sufficient generally. By and large, the mid-valley
seems to be adequately irrigated. Prolonged drought is
relatively rare during the summer.[8] The weather is in
no way as stable as it usually is in a monsoon climate.
Rapid changes are common, and the average figures
measuring the amounts of rain tend to conceal the capriciousness of the natural forces.

The relative humidity is at its highest in April when
the average figure soars to 85 per cent and it remains
above 80 per cent all through the summer. Again, autumn
and winter are much drier, with a minimum of humidity in
November, approximately 69 per cent. The changes in
temperature reflect the situation of the Colony in the
outskirts of the tropical zone. The winter monsoon
brings about a type of weather which is considerably
cooler than that dominating in Southeast Asia. The
lowest mean maximum temperature is as low as 63.4°F in
February, and the highest mean maximum in July rises to
88.9°F.[9] Typhoons and tropical storms during the summer
and autumn are much dreaded features of the Hong Kong
climate. Such storms may carry winds of a speed amounting
to some 100 m.p.h. and they strike the Colony or its
surroundings a few ·times a year. The violent force of the
wind carries with it dense rain. It sweeps away and ruins
the growing crops and causes damage to cottages and
village houses. We have already mentioned the strong
tidal waves that sometimes follow, and their destructive
effect on low-lying country. Even if today a farmer has
received warnings beforehand over the radio, there is not
much he can do to save his fields. In particular, the
gardens on the slopes are much damaged in typhoon weather.
Even in fair weather the farmers of To Fung Shan are
exposed to high winds.

The development of intense vegetable farming in the
traditional society of China seems to have been linked
to the proximity of urban central places with great
agglomerations of people. Urban marketing has, so it
seems, been a prerequisite for a one-sided specialization

on vegetable production. The spatial distribution of
horticulture has been prescribed by the culinary habits
of the Chinese. The Chinese palate demands very fresh
market goods, and any tendency of the marketed products
towards spoilage will lead to a considerable decrease of
the saleable price. Thus transportation to the city
markets must be short or rapid. As a consequence the
urban areas were often surrounded by zones of intense
horticulture. We will have more to say on this in a
later context.

During the latter half of the nineteenth century the
twin cities of Victoria and Kowloon emerged as a result
of foreign intervention and planning. Their growth was
related to the attraction the new Colony had to offer a
countryside impoverished under the strain of a rapidly
increasing population. The appearance of the new urban
districts encouraged the cultivation of cash crops in
the surrounding rural areas, which were to become the
New Territories. This development occurred within an
area with a reasonably good system of transport connecting it with the city markets. According to available information the start was made on Kowloon Peninsula
where the old villages seem to have taken advantage of
the new development quite early.[10] The continuous
spread of transport initiated after the British territorial expansion in 1898, when new roads were constructed
and the Canton-Kowloon Railway was laid out through the
district, gave rise to new opportunities and offered the
possibility to expand the zone of intense vegetable
cultivation beyond Kowloon Peninsula. The Sha Tin valley
is located just beyond the first range of mountains, but,
contrary to what one might have expected, vegetable
gardening was not to become important there until
recently in the period after the Pacific War. Obstacles
against a switch-over to horticulture may have been
found on the managerial side of production, but such
difficulties by no means account for everything. An
important barrier to change was to be found in the social
values of the village population and their knowledge
about market gardening.

Clearly an ecology of large variation demands advanced
and flexible means of accommodation if the natural re-
sources are to be fully exploited. At this point we
can see that the ecological framework is not to be
expressed in averages but in terms of the fluctuations it
displays. These, in turn, will be of great importance to
indicating upper and lower limits, both with regard to
normal and abnormal years. Ecological analysis of
horticulture will raise some basic and important questions,

such as the following. At what season is a certain
environmental factor operative? Is its effect direct
or indirect through other factors? Is it just an
indication of some other environmental feature? The
preceding pages have provided only very incomplete
answers to such questions, but a pursuit of these and
similar problems would lead to another and different
study. Our present aims are limited to a broad
presentation of the environmental and infrastructural
problems which confront the Sha Tin farmer, and the
factors we have described above may serve as a frame
of reference for our present ethnography of farming
life.

1. In the Tsuen Wan area the industrial enterprises must be described as major. For practical reasons the satellite town of Tsuen Wan will be regarded as part of the city area of Hongkong and Kowloon.
2. Freedman 1963:31ff, 1966b:9, Grant 1962, Potter 1968. More technical papers are those by Wong & Brereton and Wong & Mason, which both, to my knowledge, remain unprinted.
3. Aijmer 1967, Grant 1962.
4. Grant 1962:122.
5. Grant 1962:77f, 110.
6. An official note on the 1954 catastrophe reads:

   > The typhoons broke through the sea walls and rendered areas of agricultural land uncultivable, in particular in the Sha Tin area. The break in Pak Hok Tun sea-wall at Sha Tin has been repaired at a cost of approximately $150,000, and the land behind washed out to reduce salinity, but the loss of the crop remains where it fell (Barnett 1955:9).

   The later inundations were irreparable.
7. Grant 1962:125.
8. But for instance the summer of 1954 was unusually dry. Again, in 1963 serious drought lasted for many months causing much destruction.
9. Grant 1962:135 provides a table on the distribution of intensity of rain, maximal temperature, and sun hours.
10. This point will be further developed below.

III. MARKET GARDENING

Vegetable gardening offers such a variety of species that a full accommodation to the ecological fluctuations can be obtained. There are kinds and varieties of vegetables to suit all seasons and all soils, and the quality of the soil can to some extent be adjusted to meet the requirements of the vegetables. Attacks on crops are fought with biocides. Drought is balanced by irrigation. However, there is one variable, external to the system, which constrains the farmer's choice between different species and influences his attempts at maximization of gains within the ecosystem; this variable is the ever fluctuating market price. The vegetables and flowers which thrive during certain periods of the year are also those which are apt to fetch the lowest market price during these very periods. On the other hand, the market prices are rocked by yet other factors to which we will return in a later context. These non-environmental factors tend to make market gardening hazardous and unpredictable.

The existence of many choices accounts for the difficulty in establishing a cycle of crop rotation embracing the majority of the farmers. Charles J. Grant, in his survey, points out that

> such is the variety of vegetables grown and the rapid
> adaptations to a fluctuating market, it is difficult
> to describe a typical rotation. Indeed, some
> farmers avoid any attempt at crop rotation but grow
> Chinese white cabbage continuously, six or seven
> crops per year, every year. The more normal
> procedure is to plant according to market demand
> with a general emphasis on Chinese vegetables in the
> summer months and European-type vegetables in
> winter.[1]

We have hinted already at the fluctuation of the market; suffice it here to repeat that in the harsh world of everyday reality vegetable gardening may not be as adaptable and flexible as Grant seems to assume. It should be noted also that in the Sha Tin valley I have not come across farmers who specialize in European-type vegetables during the winter season. One exception, however, was the present vice-chairman of the Sha Tin Rural Committee, Ho Baixiung, once a farmer managing a large-scale market garden with emphasis on European species. His produce was intended for the Dairy Farm Company, which retails to a

20

mainly European or europeanized clientele. He also sold vegetables to European-style restaurants. However, Ho has discontinued this line of business.

Another example of the planting of Western vegetables, like tomatoes, is to be found on To Fung Shan where skilled gardeners work under difficult environmental conditions. Their choice of such crops is related to their remote location as tomatoes are not so perishable. Exclusive specialization in one and only one kind of vegetable, like watercress, occurs although not very frequently.

We have found that the existence of a multitude of choices accounts for the observer's difficulty in establishing a typical crop rotation shared by all farmers. It is our experience, however, that most gardeners use a cyclic combination of vegetable and flower gardening which is sometimes extended to include rice farming too. Let us consider briefly a few examples.

Wu Qiwen, who rents land close to San Tin village, cultivates flowers during the early spring. Later in spring and up to late summer he plants *sigua* - loofah or snake gourds. The latter part of the summer he plants his fields with *jiecai* - leaf mustard cabbage. During autumn and winter he cultivates *caisheng* - flowering cabbage and *baicai* - white cabbage. Yue Ling has land in the same area as Wu. He entirely special-izes in the cultivation of *xiyangcai* - water cress, maintaining a year-round crop; there are a few summer months when he has to clear his fields from the old plants and sow a new crop.

If we turn our attention to the Keng Hau area we find that Deng Fen has divided the year into two main phases. From mid-spring and onwards up to late summer he will plant his fields with loofah. Besides, from late spring through the best part of the summer he grows one crop of rice. The rest of the year he plants his land exclusively with flowers, especially *Gladiolus* and other bulbous kinds. Chen Quan thinks that a normal rotation will insure flowers in the early spring, then loofah, and later leaf mustard cabbage. In the cooler season there should be white cabbage and flowering cabbage. But he himself does not follow such a normal cycle. During spring he plants flowers, white cabbage, and flowering cabbage. Further, he sows *weibian* - string beans - which require some hundred days before they can be harvested. He takes two consecutive crops of string beans. Simultaneously with the string beans he has loofah, and a few pumpkins in one garden bed.

One of his fields is planted with watercress for the
whole year, which is to say that there is a brief interlude for clearance and resowing in the summer. The
string bean field will later be used for one crop of
flowering cabbage which requires about seventy days
before it is ready for the market. Other lots are nearly
continuously planted with flowers, mainly *Chrysanthemum*
and *Gladiolus* during the cool season, and *Celoria* during
the hot summer. In between the two flower seasons there
will be an interlude of one crop of leaf mustard cabbage.

The comparatively small farm of the Wang family is
planted with loofah and string beans during the first
half of the year, and in the latter half it is planted
with vegetables like flowering cabbage and white cabbage,
and also, at this time of the year, flowers, mostly
Chrysanthemum. Cheng Zhiming specializes entirely in
watercress farming and his fields at Keng Hau are
exclusively of this crop. Cheng has more land near the
village of Tung Lo Wan, however, but unfortunately we do
not know if this is used differently. Lu Taiyun cultivates a wide range of vegetables and flowers. The
first half of the year his fields are planted mainly
with loofah. In summer he has spring onions and later
leaf mustard cabbage. He has flowers mainly in the
autumn and winter, but fields of *Chrysanthemum* and
Celoria are to be found in the summer also. Apart
from the more common kinds he cultivates *yebiaoxiang* -
Night Fragrance - and *yinlo* - Silver Willow, both of
which are very rarely grown, and the latter requires a
whole year until it yields flowers.

Wu An is another example of a farmer who has mixed
rice production with the cultivation of flowers and,
to a lesser degree, vegetables. He only takes one
summer crop of rice. The paddy fields are later converted into flower land, mainly for *Gladiolus*. During
spring and summer there are also fields with *Chrysanthemum* and *Celoria*, and a few common vegetables like
loofah. Wei Fa has entirely specialized in flowers of
the common kinds and they are grown according to season
all through the year. The Weng family is another
example of specialization in flowers. In addition to
the flower fields they have a few trees yielding flowers
and fruit, like *bailan* - White Orchid - and *zijinghua* -
Purple Thorn Flower - and, like all farmsteads in this
area, some papaya trees.

From these examples of land use in the Sha Tin valley
we may infer something of a loose pattern of available
possibilities, a pattern which may be depicted in the
following way.[2]

Kind	J	F	M	A	M	J	J	A	S	O	N	D
Rice				—	—	—	—	—				
Loofah			—	—	—	—	—					
String beans			—	—	—	—	—	—				
Flowering cabbage	—	—	—						—	—	—	—
Leaf Mustard cabbage							—	—				
Spring onion				—	—	—	—	—	—			
Watercress	—	—	—	—	—					—	—	—
Crysanthemum		—	—	—	—	—	—	—	—	—	—	
Gladiolus	—	—	—							—	—	—
Celoria				—	—	—	—					

Thus we may discern something of a general rhythm. Spring
and early summer are dominated by loofah and string·beans.
At this time of the year the fields are covered mainly by
plants growing on structures of bamboo canes. All over
the area the view is screened by the high luxuriant
vegetation. Intermittently the eye will catch the sun's
reflection from the water of a light green field of rice
or meet the vividness of a colourful flower garden. But
the dominating impression remains the thriving deep green
walls of vegetables on bamboo trellises.

When the high growing fields are cleared in July and
August the eye is struck by the sudden change in the landscape and one enjoys a wide view over the fields, cottages
and villages. The open autumn and winter landscape
dominated by watercress and flowers, seems, in spite of
the latter, less thriving and less colourful.

The year appears to be divided into seasons in two
different ways. According to one approach, there is a
spring season beginning just after the lunar New Year in
cool weather, and ending in hot weather in August. This
is followed by an autumn season starting in September in
hot weather, which comes to an end at Christmas and the
lunar New Year. On the other hand, the year may be
thought of as one cool and dry season, and one hot and
humid season. The first alternative has its frame of
reference in the cyclical cultivation of the fields, which
means luxuriant vegetables during the first half and
flowers for the benefit of the celebration of Christmas
and New Year during the second half. The lunar New Year,
renowned for its spectacular flower markets, is especially
the natural high point and landmark for the flower
cultivation.

The alternative way to order the annual cycle reflects
the climate, but just as much it mirrors the type and
input of work into the gardens. The cool season is the
time for continuous irrigation, which, to a large extent,

is carried out manually. Even so the hot season is regarded generally as the most laborious time as the fields require an endless weeding of grass. The farmers who concentrate on the cultivation of watercress live undramatic lives doing the same sort of things all through the year. Perhaps they see a high point in the chilly winter days, when the otherwise deep green colour of the watercress leaves take on a shade of reddish hue. The produce is then at its best and will fetch the highest prices on the market.

The choice between different species of vegetables is furthermore constrained by the gardener's knowledge about the various kinds available. Most of the immigrant farmers in Sha Tin have some background knowledge of rice cultivation, at least from their childhood. In most cases rice was the main crop of their native districts, but often they have experience also of some regional specialty, like watercress, bamboo, sugar cane, and similar crops. Such technical expertise may turn out to be of importance in the immigrant's new surroundings. It is quite obvious that people in the New Territories who come from Dongguan District in China tend to cultivate watercress, a fact which is observed and frequently pointed out by the inhabitants themselves. In Sha Tin this is in no way an exclusive Dongguan feature, but there is definitely a core of Dongguan men among the watercress farmers.

Lack of technical skill in vegetable and flower growing can be helped only by the grower's learning from others in his new place of residence. In this situation he will be dependent on his new social network and the information which may be realized over this network.

An exception to this is Ye Wanzhe who has a garden, which is technically very advanced, at the bottom of the Pak Tin valley. He has specialized in a few species of flowers. All he knows about flower gardening is derived from his extensive reading on the subject and he tries to buy all books concerning floriculture he can get hold of. He takes a special interest in Japanese publications. I suspect, however, that he reads Chinese translations of Japanese originals as his knowledge of the Japanese language is very limited, if at all existent, a reminiscence only of enforced schooling during the Japanese occupation of Canton. Tan Guang, farming in the vicinity of Siu Lek Yuen, maintains that everyone can learn how to cultivate ginger flowers and *Gladiolus*. He himself is the only one - anyway in that area we may add - who has the expert knowledge required for the cultivation of more unusual kinds of seasonal flowers. Technical skill

and experience are good assets which can be converted
into cash easily as such seasonal flowers fetch a much
better price.

Vegetable gardening, as well as the cultivation of
flowers, requires an intense input of work into the
fields. The soil must be prepared. Sometimes the
fields have to be converted from dry fields into wet
fields and *vice versa*. The remains of an old crop have
to be removed and grass must be uprooted. One helpful
device in this work, which is quite common, is a simple
flame-thrower on a shaft. The farmer walks over his
field burning away all undesirable vegetation. This
efficient implement is fairly cheap (the price was
around HK$40 in 1969). Almost every farm has got one
flame-thrower and the gardeners who are not in the
possession of one can easily borrow. When using this
device one has to be quite cautious. Paraffin may
easily flow out on the ground and the soil will be destroyed on that spot. Often flame-throwers are used
only when grass and weeds are thick and thriving. The
implement is regarded as not very durable; it tends to
break only after a few seasons' use. When the remainder
of an old crop of a field is cleared away, the whole
family joins in the work. The small children pull out
the wilting flower-stalks with their hands and carry off
the heaps of waste. The men will turn the soil with
long hoes and the women hack the cakes of earth with
curved knives, long hoes, and rakes. Generally the
fields are worked by hand with traditional tools.

Sometimes ploughing is considered a necessity. A
few farmers have their own cows to which are given the
task of draught animals. In the Keng Hau area four
immigrant households keep cows - those of Deng Fen,
Ou Xi, Wei Fa, and Weng Guiyou. Small groups of cows
are seen roaming along the paths of Sha Tin and are
driven home in the evenings by shrill-voiced women.
Most of these animals belong to the indigenous villagers.
Water buffaloes are nowadays comparatively rare in this
area. When a village farmer needs a cow for ploughing
he will contact a friend of his who is in the possession
of one. But he must know this friend quite well and there
must be mutual trust: "Otherwise the owner would not rely
on it that his cow would not be overworked".

It seems as if similar possibilities are at hand for
the immigrant farmers, although the set of cow-owners who
are potential animal-lenders will be much more limited
for an outsider. However, we cannot exclude the possibility that such work assistance can be hired at a fee,
although we have not found any actual cases to give

substance to assumptions in this direction. Most vegetable growers are capable of managing even heavy work
manually. The cultivation of rice requires ploughing
though. Only one of the immigrant farmers in the Keng
Hau area who takes a crop of rice has a cow, and this
is Deng Fen; but Wu An may borrow Deng's cow whenever he
needs it as the two are very close in other respects;
among other things they share a diesel pump.

The land is shaped into high garden beds separated by
small irrigation furrows. The clods of earth are cut
into a fine texture with long hoes. Those garden beds
have to be repaired constantly. The earth of the sharp,
clearcut sides tends to fall down into the water furrows
and this must not happen. This work, like most other
toil concerned with vegetables and flowers, is executed
as individual labour on most occasions. Each tenant
cares for his own land only. We have been told that a
farmer may get a helping hand from neighbours, for
instance for the harvesting of a field when time is
precious, and we believe that this may occur occasionally;
tho social implications of such assistance are not
altogether clear.

Traditionally the arable land was supplied with water
by way of a complex system of irrigation, which carried
water from the brooks and mountain streams down to the
terraced fields which could be inundated one by one in a
set order. When one field has been filled or has
obtained a sufficient supply, the water is made to pass
on to the next, from which it will be transferred to yet
another field. If there is a shortage of water this will
mean that the lower-lying fields are supplied with less
water than those on the higher terraces. However, small
canals between the dykes feed the water directly and
independently into lower areas where it may be stored in
tanks or small pools. This system was designed for wet-
rice cultivation and insofar as it can be judged today
it was very efficient. But it was also the foremost
source of conflict between villages and between villagers.

This traditional irrigation system now supplies the
vegetable and flower growers with water. Naturally, the
frequent showers of the wet summertime provide water
directly, but even in this season the fields are dependent on the water carried in the irrigation system. When
someone rents a piece of land, his tenancy rights are
accompanied by corresponding rights to the irrigation
system, which means that it is open to anyone with such
rights to conduct water to his rented fields.

The water in the dug-out furrows flows around the
high garden beds and the earth absorbs moisture. The

irrigation is sufficient for many kinds of vegetables
like the important loofah. But often there is also a
further need for a direct sprinkling of the garden beds.
For many plants and flowers this is achieved by way of
splashing the water by hand from the irrigation furrows
between the beds.

   A small water storage in the vicinity of the fields
is an important asset for the market gardener. Normally
the plantations have to be watered three times a day if
showers of rain do not eliminate this strenuous work.
The ordinary procedure is that water is collected from
such a storage pool in two wooden barrels supplied with
long spouts. The farmer walks down a few concrete
steps into the pool; there he squats in the water until
the pair of barrels, which he carries on a pole over his
back, have been filled. Then he jogs back to the nearby
field where he sprinkles the water by powerful movements
up and down so that the water is spread in a thin film
over vegetables and flowers. It is important that the
water is sprinkled in such a way that it will not run
off so rapidly that the soil is carried away and damage
caused to the garden bed.

   Most plants grown are irrigated in this fashion,
among them aquatic kinds like watercress which has to be
soaked several times a day to maintain the freshness of
the leaves. Each time this is done the farmer has to
perform a considerable amount of work. Two barrels of
water are called one *danshui* - 'a pole-burden of water'.
Yue Ling, for example, farming near San Tin, estimates
that each day he will have to carry and distribute some
two hundred *danshui* on to his watercress fields. Ma Hua
in Pak Tin evaluates the numbers of *danshui* to more than
one hundred each time, and the fields require generally
three waterings a day.

   In the Keng Hau area all farmers make use of the
water carried in the irrigation system. In other areas
where this advantage is not at hand other means have to
be found. It is apparent that a most effective device
to secure a supply of water is the digging of a well.
But a new well is an expensive project, the prerequisite for which is a long-term investment plan for the
land. Chen Quan had the good fortune to find that a
well was already in existence in one of the fields he
was going to rent when he arrived to the Keng Hau area.
He paid the owner of that piece of land HK$200 once and
for all for the use of this facility. Unfortunately
Chen's land is very scattered and the value of the well
is therefore diminished. Deng Fen is the owner of two
wells which have been dug on his own initiative. The

cost for these two exceeded one thousand dollars. Lu
Taiyun has constructed an unusually sizeable well. The
opening measures six by six *chi* and it is 22 *chi* deep.
His costs for this installation were more than one
thousand dollars.

Probably it is the high costs which cause more farmers
to refrain from digging wells, especially if the advantage of a well is balanced against the access to other
sources of water. One way to compensate for the absence
of a traditional irrigation system is to lead water in
pipelines from mountain brooks or constructed water
tanks on the hillside to storage pools or field-side
tanks. Thus Chen Han in the Yue Yuen area takes his
water from a pipe issuing from a big villa-like structure
in the vicinity, in front of which there is a big pool.
On the slopes of To Fung Shan many people take advantage
of the natural pressure of running water, which is conducted through an extensive system of pipes to tanks
located among the terraced fields.

However, a more common device is to pump water into
storages. Small diesel pumps transfer water from ditches
and brooks to collection pools in strategic positions,
from where it can be sprinkled manually over the garden
beds. Again, the price is an important barrier for widespread use. A pump will cost nearly one thousand dollars,
and in any case not less than HK$700. They will be used
during the dry season mainly. Of eight pump owners in the
Keng Hau area six have low-lying fields in *xialu* - the
land on the lower side of the main path through the Keng
Hau area.

A few sophisticated and enterprising gardeners, like
Ye Wanzhe in Pak Tin and several on the slopes of To Fung
Shan, have acquired sprinkler installations for a mechan-
ical and efficient irrigation of the fields. The
sprinkler devices are fed with water from concrete tanks
by way of plastic hoses, and the gadget is operated by
the natural water pressure. These gardeners still experiment with different types of sprinklers. Such innovations
eliminate a great deal of manual work as the sprinklers
may be placed out on the fields so nearly every corner is
reached by their cascades.

The sowing of seeds and the planting of flower bulbs is
an important but undramatic phase of the garden cultivation. The main problem connected with this period is
the number of sparrows which feed in the paddy fields
generally. At the sowing they may invade the farmer's
garden in large flocks. Attempts are made to keep the
sparrows away, for instance by the construction of a low
horizontal framework of bamboo with crossed canes, which

makes it difficult for the birds to come down to the surface and reach the seeds. Other devices to frighten the sparrows are common. They vary from the use of rags and paper sheets attached to sticks stuck down in the earth to Chen Quan's scare-crow, with coat and hat, a polythene-bag banner in one hand, and a dead sparrow in the other.

Many vegetables and flowers are transplanted in order to obtain a better result. Although it may not be entirely necessary most farmers prefer to do so even if it increases the burden of work. When the transplantation is to be carried out depends on the kind of plant but usually it is done when the first leaves have appeared and the plants are still very small. They are transferred to new fields where they are spread out with a few inches' distance in between. Watercress is transplanted also and there is only need to sow one field which may later be used as a nursery from which shoots are taken and planted in other fields. Once the shoots are stuck into the earth under water they form roots quickly, and their growth is rapid.

Wu Qiwen in the San Tin neighbourhood does not transplant his vegetables and flowers. He is of the opinion that transplantation does not make any significant difference and that weeding is a sufficient method. However, Wu is disabled; he has only one arm and he walks with a limp. Perhaps his unwillingness to transplant is related to this and a wish to eliminate this phase of the work.

Another prerequisite for the cultivation of many kinds of vegetables is the erection of bamboo structures; generally trellis units of four canes in rows with ends tied together. There are many other ways to arrange the bamboo sticks in accordance with the needs of different plants. The canes must be bought and they are generally imported from Taiwan. Other kinds of vegetables and flowers need smaller supporting sticks.

In horticulture and floriculture each species demands its own special treatment and care. The growth of the plant must be under meticulous control. Fertilizing is an important part of this process. The fertilizers applied to the soil are of many different kinds. Of the artificial types one most commonly used is called *hongwan* - 'red pills'. It comes in the form of "rice grains but in red colour". Of non-artificial fertilizers the most common are *guhui* - 'bone ash' - and *mahui* -'hemp ash' (but in fact groundnut cakes - the remains after the pressing of oil), but the farmer may also use such materials as ashes, duck feathers, and lime. *Mahui* is regarded as the most reliable

29

of these and it is much better than artificial chemical fertilizers. The effect of natural fertilizers is longer than that obtained by the use of chemicals. The latter are regarded as more expensive, although they cost less on the market, as they have to be reapplied constantly. According to the farmers the artificial fertilizers may also cause the produce to take on a slightly bitter taste.

Such fertilizers are bought in the shops of Sha Tin Market. I have only found one example of the use of a shop in Tai Wai. Its existence, however, suggests that the farmers of the Tai Ling area - the hinterland of Tai Wai - make use of its facilities. These shops are in the style of country stores and keep stocks comprising a wide range of items, from canned food, cigarettes, and soft drinks to fertilizers, chicken feed, and vegetable seeds. There is good reason to return to these shops later. The farmer must be careful about what is de- livered. One merchant of Sha Tin Market is reputed to mix the fertilizers he sells with other materials to extract more profit from his trade. Of course, in such a case they not only become less effective, but they may even prove harmful as they cause the earth to cake.

The best fertilizer a farmer can apply to his field is nightsoil. Mainly this is delivered from the city area and is carried out to the New Territories to storage depots, which are under the administration of the cooperative societies and the Department of Agri- culture and Fisheries. This scheme was launched in 1952. The distribution apparatus is in the hands of the Urban Council of Hong Kong Government.[3] The farmer can buy the amount he needs at the depot at a price of two dollars a *dan* - 'picul'. The fertilizer is carried from the depot to special manure pits situated among the fields. Most gardeners make use of their own supply and have private latrines among the fields - a pit surrounded by tin sheets to give a bit of privacy.[4]

The different fertilizers are used strategically in relation to crops and time. Those mentioned above are suitable for most plants and generally there is no need for changes and many farmers stick to the same stuff all the time. The powder is applied directly, or more commonly, mixed with water, soon after the first shoots have appeared. But a more professional approach involves changes. For instance, the string beans are allowed to grow on their bamboo trellis until they reach the height of four *chi*. Then the fertilizers are applied, preferably *mahui*. When the pods appear it is time for nightsoil.

Nightsoil is regarded also as the best fertilizer to
be used at transplantations.

The rotation of crops is another way to improve the
soil. Particularly, the farmers who cultivate one crop
of rice do this explicitly in order to improve the
fields for the cultivation of flowers in the autumn.
There is a general opinion that floriculture makes the
earth salty and a repetitive cultivation of flowers on
the same plot of land will eventually bring about a low
quality produce. However, the insertion of one crop of
rice will, so we are told, eliminate all undesirable
salinity from the soil.

The use of insecticides is a neccesity for the
gardener and they are constantly applied to the crops.
Already a few days after the sowing the first spraying
is done. The insecticide is distributed over the field
by way of shots from a simple hand spray in the form of
a tube, or by way of a somewhat more complicated device
known as a knapsack sprayer which atomizes the fluid
into a fine mist. The flow is kept constant by keeping
a high pressure in the container which is continuously
pumped with the left hand. The knapsack sprayer appears
in different forms but is usually carried by a strap
over the shoulders. Generally insecticides are sprayed
in the evening just after sunset. This is because the
insects come out during the night while they spend the
days hidden in the foliage.

We must mention one special installation. Ye Wanzhe
in Pak Tin, to whom we have referred above because of
his technically advanced garden farm, has introduced a
project for his flower beds, which is unique in Sha Tin.
In the evening he turns on a set of electric bulbs hung
up over the fields. The flowers grow in constant light
day and night which increases their rate of growth. Ye
claims he got the idea for his installation from his
studies of Japanese discourses on floriculture.

Cutting grass on the dykes between the fields and
repairing garden beds are time-consuming tasks. Weeding
is another endless toil. Flowers like *Chrysanthemum*
must have their stalks cleared of green leaves. The
work in the fields is very intense for every crop
throughout the year.

It is estimated that each field, provided that the
weather conditions are good, can yield six or seven
crops in a year. The input of work is divided between
the fields in such a fashion that while the soil is
prepared, garden beds built, and sowing done in some
fields, other lots are harvested. All vegetables and
flowers are cut with a small thumb knife - a sharp

blade in the form of a ring to be worn on the thumb. This knife provides the advantage that both hands are free during the work and the plant can be held and cut with the same hand. The work is exhausting, especially so for the watercress farmers who have to squat on a board laid out on the marshy field and cut the small plants one by one with the thumb knife for many and consecutive hours.

Before they can harvest they must water their fields to make the leaves more crisp and easier to cut. This procedure adds to the strain of the work. Once the watercress has grown to a suitable size the fields can be cut over and over again. Other crops may also have a prolonged harvest; for instance, string beans are cut during a period of some twenty days. The harvest is no short and dramatic high point marking off the end of a long period of growth in the fields.

At harvest vegetables are tied with bast into bunches, or they are collected into big plaited bamboo baskets, as a preparation for the marketing. When flowers are cut they are tied up into small bundles of about ten.

In this way the everyday activities of the vegetable and flower grower proceed as an uneventful flow of technical acts. Life is not always dull, but moments of excitement have little to do with market gardening. Social drama has its roots elsewhere.

NOTES TO CHAPTER III

1. Grant 1962:122.
2. This cycle is largely confirmed by the papers by
   Wong & Brereton and Wong & Mason, as well as by
   Osgood 1975, I, 151 ff.
3. For further information on this scheme see Barrow
   1951:4.
4. This is all very traditional in Chinese farming
   life; see for instance Kulp 1925:58f.

IV. INVESTMENTS, EXPENDITURES AND EFFORTS

If we turn our attention to the economic aspects of
gardening, we must first declare that the data in our
possession will in no way satisfy the rural economist.
One main reason for this is that potential informants
are often very suspicious when it comes to a discussion
of incomes and expenditures. This is something which
definitely belongs to the sphere of privacy and it is
not a matter for display. Another reason is that there
is no book-keeping and accounting. The figures provided
are estimates and approximations and they represent
ideas, a summing-up of experience, rather than figures
standing for what actually has been paid and received.
Thus we cannot present our findings with any pretensions
that they are of a definite character. Nor can we claim
that our description will cover all economic activities
of the farming community of the Sha Tin valley. But
granted these failures in our collection of data, we
think that, nevertheless, it will provide us with some
insight into the processes of economics and economic
thought.

The lack of accounting and the lack of interest for
exactness in economic questions seem to us to be linked
to a characteristic Chinese informal approach to
economy very different from the formal and technical
approach pertaining to Western European countries for
instance, characterized by a clear and systematized
consciousness of prices, interests, profits, and so on,
expressed in forms of bills, contracts, receipts, and
many other written items. Of course, it is not to be
denied that a technical economic apparatus exists also
in the economically highly sophisticated Chinese
society, but we will argue that such systematic knowledge is less widespread there than in the West and
largely confined to urban circles. Even there oral
agreements and undocumented trust are important features
of the business life.

Regarding the quality of the collection of data it is
interesting to note that Jack M. Potter experienced
similar difficulties in his field-work in the Ping Shan
area of the New Territories. Professor Potter writes:

> The vegetable farmers themselves do not keep any
> systematic records of their expenses and profits, and
> they have difficulty even remembering how much they
> made from a given crop in the previous year. When
> asked to give an estimate of the average profit made

34

on one d.c. *(douzhong)* of vegetable land a year, most farmers flatly refused, saying that there were simply too many variables involved. In fact, the village farmers said that it was impossible to construct a reasonably accurate picture of the average profits made in vegetables.[1]

One of the most important investments for the immigrant farmer in Sha Tin is the rent he has to pay for his land. The sum varies according to the estimated productivity of the soil, the access to water and, as it seems, the landlord's opinion of what is a reasonable price.[2] In the Siu Lek Yuen area we are told that one *douzhong*, or one *dou* - the short-form being the one in general use - usually will cost HK$300 per year. In the village of Kak Tin the corresponding figure is HK$200, but the variation in prices is striking. Wu Qiwen, who rents his fields from Kak Tin, pays HK$500 for two *dou*.

In our more systematic investigation of the Keng Hau area we found that sixteen households were willing to give some information on their land holdings. The areas under cultivation are, without exception, counted in terms of *dou*. But there is no exactness, and estimates are phrased like "about four *dou*" or "more than four *dou*". Again, it is difficult to know whether the word *dou* refers to the official *douzhong* of the Colony of one sixth of an acre, the much smaller local Sha Tin *douzhong*, or just to a field surrounded by dikes.[3] Information on rent is given in a similarly vague terminology. The estimates of landholdings of the immigrants were checked against the land records in the Tai Po District Office[4] to provide a more rigid framework. This procedure has underscored the vagueness of our field data.

We can table the results of our inquiry in the Keng Hau neighbourhood as shown below.

The households of Wang and Cheng have only two *dou* each. Wang Bei works in a factory and he is only a part-time farmer. Ou Xi and Cheng Zhiming have more land elsewhere. Weng Guiyou has, as was mentioned above, added a piece of unleased Crown Land to his farm. It was not yet under cultivation in the late summer of 1969.

We may compare our unsatisfactory findings with those of Ray Giles and Yung Wai Chung who conducted a social survey of Sha Tin in 1966. Information was collected from 32 'households' and the figures arrived at for area of land rented run from 231 square feet ($\frac{1}{3}$ *dou*) to 18,500,000 square feet (2,466 official

Household	Estimated area in *douzhong*	Rent paid in HK$	Actual size in acres	HK$/acre
Deng Fen	about 6	about 600*	1.0	ca.860
Ou	more than 6	a few hundred**	0.1 in Keng Hau	?
Chen Quan	about 4	about 575	0.3	ca.1,920
Zhao	more than 4	over 700	?	?
Wang	2		0.2	?
Zeng Fu	more than 4		0.3	?
Zeng Chengda	more than 4	about 1,100	0.2	ca.5,500
Chen Meigui	3	350	0.1	ca.3,500
Xie	more than 4	about 520	0.2	ca.2,600
Cheng	2	450	0.4 in Keng Hau	ca.1,120
Lu	about 6	2,160	0.8	ca.2,700
Lo	?	?	1.0	?
Deng Shouhua	more than 5	over 700	0.6	ca.1,160
Wu	6	over 1,000	0.3	ca.3,330
Wei	over 4	about 1,000	0.3	ca.3,330
Weng Guiyou	4	about 800	0.2	ca.4,000
Weng Risheng	?	?	0.4	?
Huang	4-5	quite cheap	0.2	?

douzhong). The statistical treatment of this survey
does not explain these vast differences. Similar
variations are to be found in the computation of rates
of rent. The extremes are HK$1.20 and HK$4,040.00 in
a sample of 30 pieces of land! It is concluded that
rent collected does not seem to relate to the area of
land, for there are great differences in rent. Thus,
it is said, it must relate to other factors. The
guess of the authors is that the variation might refer
to rising land values and that land contracted more
recently would require a higher rent to be paid. Even
if the figures were accurate they do not lend themselves easily to a simple explanation.[5]

However vague our own figures are, they give us
some idea about the variability of the rents paid for
land. It is obvious, of course, that data such as we
present here have little to do with orthodox economic
analysis, although we feel that they are very close
to social reality. The somewhat more reliable figures
(in an empiricist's sense) computed by us show a
variation from something like HK$1,000 per acre to
HK$5,500 per acre. Asking questions about these
differences the Keng Hau informants referred to factors
such as the quality of soil, irrigation, existence of
white ants, and similar features, to account for the
variation in price. Again, it appears that the whim of
the landlord is important.

Generally land rent is paid in two installments and
in advance. The procedure as such appears undramatic
and non-ritualized. "Sometimes I go to the landowner's
house to pay when I have got the money, sometimes the
landowner comes here to collect his money," explains
Deng Shouhua. We are told that in the Kak Tin area
land rents were flexible earlier, and they were
calculated in accordance with the yields of the crops.
Later on the sums became fixed. When this change was
introduced remains unclear. One interesting case in
the Keng Hau neighbourhood is Zeng Chengda who pays
his rent in rice grain, and he delivers 600 catties of
unhusked rice per year and *dou*. He buys the grain in
Sha Tin Market. Thus his land rent is changing all
the time in accordance with the price of rice on the
market. Generally he has to pay about 40 cents per
catty, but in 1967, in the wake of the summer riots in
the Colony, the price was up to 60 cents which is the
highest he ever paid. We shall return to this case in
a later context.[6]

The immigrant farmers who have occupied unleased
Crown Land may, to some extent, get compensation for

their less productive soil - such land is generally
situated on the hillsides - by the fact that they do
not have to pay rent for their fields. Only a minor
fee is paid to the District Office for an occupancy
license.[7] As has been mentioned above, Weng Guiyou,
who farms in the neighbourhood of Keng Hau, is the
only person there who has taken up new Crown Land, of
about half a *dou* in size.

It has been said earlier that when a gardener rents
land he will obtain simultaneous rights to the irrigation system which serves that land. Thus water is
not generally connected with expenses and investments.
On the other hand, there is a wish to stabilize
production by way of offsetting the capriciousness of
the weather. We have described already new forms of
irrigation which have been applied in connexion with
horticulture and floriculture. These new devices,
like pumps and mechanic sprinklers, are combined with
the construction of traditional wells and water tanks.
However, it is fairly expensive to dig a well. In the
Keng Hau area Deng Fen has dug two wells, the costs of
which surpassed HK$1,000. Likewise, Ou Xi has two
wells, one for drinking water and the other for irrigation purposes. He claims he constructed the wells
himself, but it seems as if expertise is required
generally for the work. Chen Quan has paid a fee of
HK$200 for the use of a well already existing in his
rented fields.

Lu Taiyun has got an unusually deep well, the costs
of which amounted to over HK$1,000. Lu made the
decision to invest this large amount of money in the
summer of 1964 during the great drought of that year.
Other people like the two Zeng, Weng, Wei and Wang have
wells also, but as far as we know these were not constructed by the tenants; if they were, the work was not
connected with high costs. All of these wells are
supplied with water by small streams. In this area it
seems as if well-digging was the concern of those
farmers who have land of about six *dou* or so. Both
Deng and Lu belong to this category. Wu An, whose farm
is of a smaller size, is furthermore in the position to
take advantage of Deng Fen's two wells. Lo Cai has
another sizeable farm, and there is a well in his
fields. His total refusal to communicate with anthropologists has left us in uncertainty about this installation. However, it seems reasonable to suggest that
unless a farmer has access to a considerable piece of
land he is not prone to invest in well-digging.

Pumps are important devices to fight drought conditions, especially during the dry winter season. One informant expressed himself thus: "To be a farmer you are supposed to have a pump at least." Still the idea behind this statement is remote from the observable reality. In the Keng Hau area we know of eight households in the possession of a pump. Two of these households, those of Deng Fen and Wu An, share one pump. The other six are those of Ou, Zhao, Zeng Fu, Lu, Wei, and Weng. The cost of a pump would amount to at least HK$700 (in 1969). That Deng Fen and Lu should have pumps was only to be expected with regard to the size of their farming enterprises. As mentioned, Wu has a share in the Deng pump to make it even more useful. Whether Lu has one we do not know.

In the Keng Hau area it is generally assumed that the portion of land known as *shanglu* - 'above the path' - has better water conditions than *xialu* -'beneath the path'. The water of the mountain streams is led through the irrigation system; first it is conducted through *shanglu*, and only when the fields there have had their full supply will the water be passed on to *xialu*. Of the farmers possessing land in *xialu*, the Huang household does not have a pump, nor have the Wang, Chen Meigui, and Chen Quan households. Of these holdings Huang's piece of land in the fields beneath the path is at the very side of a water ditch. The Wang household has but a small farm largely managed by its women. They have a well within easy reach. The land belonging to Chen Meigui is small also and mainly managed by the old woman herself with some assistance from her daughter in the evenings.

Chen Quan's land here is about the same size as that of the Wang household, and he has a well. Furthermore we understand that Chen may borrow a pump from Lu should he feel a strong need. We are doubtful about the Liu and Yuan households. They have only a small parcel of land here and it is possible that they may borrow their close neighbour Ou's pump, although they are not otherwise particularly friendly.

These data seem to suggest that the purchase of a pump involves a rational calculation, in which the benefits of irrigation are balanced against costs relating to risks of drought, size of farm, production ambitions, and management. In *shanglu* there is a good supply of water under normal conditions. Still, small farmers like those of Zeng Fu, Wei, and Weng have pumps. Their fields are located near water ditches and they have wells within easy reach. This does not fit in

with that suggestion. Thus we must look for other
possibilities to explain the distribution of pumps.

One alternative has been suggested by Jack Potter.
We do not feel inclined to make use of Potter's
argument, however, that the innovation of pumps was
probably adopted, not merely for utilitarian reasons,
but also as prestige symbols.[8] Potter's conclusion is
well-founded in his own ethnography, but there is
nothing to suggest that this statement applies to the
Sha Tin situation. But if we glance through the list
of pump owners we will notice that they are all early
settlers in the Keng Hau area.[9] We believe that this
fact has had a bearing on their irrigation strategy.
When they started their farming here only part of the
land was leased to outsiders, and a significant proportion was still under the rice cultivation of native
villagers. In these early days there was frequent
quarrelling between village farmers and outsider
farmers about water. That rights to water should go
with rights to land was apparently not a clearly established rule then. Both sides felt that the other
party encroached on their rights in this respect. As
a response to the malicious water policy of the
indigenous rice farmers, and in order to relieve themselves of the strains of 'water terrorism', the early
immigrant settlers invested in pumps. Late-comers did
not have to face the water problem in the atmosphere
of the hostility of citizenship-minded villagers.
However, water still gives rise to problems, a topic
we will deal with elsewhere.

We are badly informed as to the costs of the more
sophisticated sprinkler irrigation employed by some
farmers in Pak Tin and on To Fung Shan. It is
evident, however, that this sophistication is based
largely on, and is dependent on, the co-operation and
financial support of the Department of Agriculture.
In practice, not all peasants have equal chances to
obtain such benefits. Suffice it to note here that we
have not come across one single farmer in the Sha Tin
valley proper conducting experiments with sprinkler
devices. Of course, this fact has to be balanced
against the existence there of old irrigation systems.

A farmer needs a number of tools, like ploughs, hoes,
knives, buckets, carrying poles, and bamboo canes. A
considerable amount of money is laid down on this
collection of implements. It is generally accepted in
the area that the prices for agricultural tools have
gone up considerably in recent years. Thus a set of

2. Wang Di selling loofah in Sha Tin market

farming utensils increase more and more in value. Lu
Tai Yun in the Keng Hau area, who has a six *dou* farm,
makes the rough estimate that his tools nowadays are
worth some HK$2,000. This figure will then include a
diesel pump at perhaps HK$700, a flame-thrower at
HK$40, a couple of insecticide sprayers at perhaps
HK$50,and a vast amount of bamboo canes imported from
Taiwan and sold at 15 cents each. The capital which is
invested in farming tools varies from farm to farm, and
it is not possible, nor useful, to form a more definite
opinion on this matter.

If we now turn from the farmer's basic investments
to his current expenditures we will find that, on the
whole, these go into the shops of Sha Tin Market and
Tai Wai. We have only encountered one farmer, in Tin
Sam, who actually frequents the shops in Tai Wai but
obviously the shops there cater for the most part for
the nearby surroundings - the Tai Ling area. Sha Tin
Market is much more important commercially for most
gardeners, and they frequently go there. On these
expeditions they do their business with the shops.

Fertilizers are one of the most important expenditures of the farmer. The better kind, *mahui*, will
cost 60 cents a catty, where chemical stuff is sold at
half that price, 30 cents per catty. They come in
paper bags of 70 catties. Nightsoil is bought from the
Co-operative Society depot for two dollars per *dan* -
'picul'. But today it has lost much of its former
importance. Mostly private latrines account for its
continued use. The farmers who keep animals like pigs
and cows are careful to save their droppings. Insecticides are equally important items for current expenses.
They are bought from two specially licensed shops in Sha
Tin Market. They cost HK$4-4.50 for a container of
100cc.

What are the actual costs of the farmer? It is
recognised that it is very difficult to estimate in what
quantities insecticides and fertilizers are used. This
is especially so in the summer when the frequent rains
wash away what has been spread out and sprayed. They
have to be reapplied constantly. It is said that these
investments are more dependent on the weather than on
the kind of crop. Wei Chunshang, a Tin Sam vegetable
and flower grower, says his investments in fertilizers
and insecticides for a year for his five *dou* farm is at
least one thousand dollars. Chen Quan, in the Keng Hau
neighbourhood, is aware that every time he sprays his
string bean field of half a *dou,* it will cost him some
two dollars. But he has no idea of how many times he

has to spray during the 100 days' period of growth for
one crop. Naturally, there are also variations between
different kinds of crops. Vegetables generally require
more fertilizers and insecticides than flowers. For
instance, Wei Chunshang of Tin Sam grows more flowers
than vegetables. The reason for this preference is
partly the lower investments required for flowers.
Vegetables are more demanding and "certain periods of
the year one has to apply enormous quantities of insecticides and fertilizers. If not, the vegetables would be
eaten up by insects in two or three days."

Weng Guiyou, of the Keng Hau area, who specializes in
flowers, estimates his total costs in this respect to be
some HK$200 per *dou* a year, whereas Ou Xi, who has a
mixed vegetable and flower garden, indicates that he
spends more than HK$300 on the same unit for the same
time. Chen Quan gives a figure as low as HK$130 per
dou for vegetables. For his half-*dou* string bean field
his estimate is much higher though. For each crop –
and there will be two of them in the first half of the
year – he spends about HK$100. This means about 200
dollars for this small parcel of land in about two
hundred days. After the beans he takes two crops of
flowering cabbage, which adds further to the total
expenditure laid down on this lot. On the other hand,
loofah requires much less fertilizing.

The same uncertainty applies to the costs of seeds.
They are generally 'very cheap', but flower bulbs for
Gladiolus for instance, which are imported from Japan
and Holland, are more expensive. Again, the totally
informal way of handling economic data leaves us with
little useful economic information.

Spending and investing form a continuous process of
allocation of available money, which becomes complex
to the farmer of a diversified garden. Day by day he is
exposed to the necessity of giving out money for different reasons, and these reasons do not necessarily form
one meaningful unit. It seems to us that a systematic
knowledge is beyond reach mainly because the farmer
tends to split up his economic thinking into separate
provinces, isolating each single crop on each single
landlot. Thus he may be surrounded by four or five
sets of continuous events, and these sets are not
integrated in his mind, nor are they embraced by one
process of overall rational economic calculation.
Furthermore, it seems to us that the key factor deter-
mining the economic fate of a farmer lies in his mental
capability of arriving at a more systematized and
integrated knowledge of the flow of money in his farming

business. To us it is significant that more successful
farmers like Ye Wanzhe in Pak Tin, Deng Fen and Lu
Taiyun in the Keng Hau area have a businessman or shop
clerk background.[10] Such experience has an urban or
market town genesis. It is characterized by the
clicking sounds of the abacus.

We have found similar difficulties in our attempts
at securing figures for the vegetable and flower
grower's returns. These difficulties are founded in
the fluctuating market prices and the differences
between the degree of profit-making pertaining to the
different market places. We shall deal with the
marketing processes in some detail in what follows.
Incomes vary also with the type of marketed produce and
with the seasons. What the anthropologist can gain by
research in the field is on the one hand approximations
of how much a family will need for its subsistence, and
on the other, ideas about how much money they generally
receive.

The Lu household in the Keng Hau neighbourhood consists of three adults and six children of varying age.
For their subsistence they need a daily income of
about HK$30. The daily gains from the six *dou* farm
vary from HK$10-20 in the worst season, which is summer,
and up to as much as HK$60 in the spring. Lu Taiyun
maintains that his monthly income will never be below
HK$500, even if he has bad luck, but that he often earns
much more. The household of Chen Quan consists of three
adults and four younger children. They make a living by
farming four *dou* of land, plus the salary of the oldest
daughter who works in a factory in town. Chen Quan
estimates the needs of the family to be at least HK$10 a
day from the farm. Sometimes in the summer he only gets
eight dollars. It is very fluctuating. A general estimate, which we have heard very frequently, is that a
gardener will usually earn about HK$1,000 per *dou* a year.
This seems to be a reasonable estimate of a minimal
income, although it comes from both specialized flower
growers, mixed flower-vegetable gardeners, as well as
from watercress specialists. A household with a number
of children will need an income of about HK$15 a day to
meet their basic needs and expenditures. Farming households which depend entirely on the output of the land
will rarely rely on an area smaller than four *dou*. This
means that one can gain nearly three dollars a day from
each *dou*; and four *dou*, then, provides an income of
about HK$12 a day. Thus, given the vast stretch of the
fluctuation of prices, the estimate makes a good deal of
sense. Presumably it is a somewhat conservative figure

and we are inclined to believe that it stands for the
minimal yield of a year. With a bit of luck the gains
will be higher.

The sociological survey of Sha Tin of 1966, mentioned
above, states that the expenses for an average squatter
in Sha Tin, calculated on a monthly basis, and on the
median average, total HK$77.60. This figure is not too
far removed from our own estimates. The same survey
lists 11 village 'families' engaged in cash crop farming.
It approximates the total annual return from the sale
to HK$36,560 which gives an average income of HK$3,323
per 'family'. Assuming a standard four *dou* farm, this
figure is not that far from our conservative estimates.
It is not altogether clear to us how the conductors of
the survey could secure these figures.[11]

To exemplify further we may return to Chen Quan's
string bean field. This produces about 400 catties in
one crop. Harvest lasts for about 20 days; Chen will be
selling the beans in Sha Tin Market and have a return of
some HK$20 a day during this period. In two hundred
days of spring and summer, this half-*dou* will give him
an income of about HK$800. Some years watercress culti-
vation turns out to be very profitable. Chen Quan's
half-*dou* of watercress land was extremely profitable a
few years ago, when the produce fetched a price of
80 cents-$1 per catty. He claims that during the long
season they could cut 1,000 catties per month. Even if
this is a good round figure, it is obvious that watercress farming was well worthwhile.

Naturally the incomes are not only to cover the input
into the farm but also food, clothing, housing, transportation, extra labour, education, and amusements.
Food is frugal congee or rice with some *sung* - 'accompani-
ment' - of duck, chicken, fish and vegetables. Some of
this comes from the farmer's own fowl and his own gardens.
Clothing is limited to T-shirt and shorts for men, or a
traditional suit of jacket and wide trousers. Women
sport blouses and long trousers, or traditional suits
with aprons. Winter and summer may call for different
materials. Men and women alike use plastic sandals, cloth
gym shoes, and rubber boots. For protection from the sun
many men use colonial style topees made of plastic.
Women generally wear traditional wide-brimmed plaited hats.
Children are poorly dressed in remade old pieces of
clothing.

Housing is also connected with spending. If a man
lives in a hut on Crown Land or on rented agricultural
land, his main cost for housing will be 'tea money',
bribes paid to the police-like squatter patrols if the
house is an illegal one, which is often the case.

There are some initial expenses for the construction of a residential hut; the costs connected with this vary tremendously owing to the size and the standard chosen by the builder. It is difficult to arrive at good figures for such expenses. Often a dwelling of this kind emerges in stages by way of additions and extensions, and even the farmers themselves are unaware of the total sum of their expenditures. Again, prices have risen constantly during the last decades, and this fact makes a simple summing up of costs for materials and services, widely dispersed in time, less meaningful.

However, we have some information on how Chen Quan in Keng Hau erected his illegal structure in 1967. The building materials cost him over HK$1,000. In addition to this he had to hire workers and pay off the squatter-control inspector as a license for a temporary structure was not granted by the District Office. He estimates his total input into this project to be some HK$3,000. In 1969, the squatter inspector asked him for an additional sum of 'tea money' of HK$800, but Chen was reluctant to pay this sum for different reasons. Chen had to borrow money for this house construction which was possible through relatives of his wife in Hongkong and Kowloon. In 1969, two years later, he still owed them some HK$2,000. Chen's house is a wooden one. Had he preferred a 'stone cottage' of concrete the cost would have amounted to four times as much as he paid for the present dwelling.[12]

We must draw attention also to the fact that some households remit money back to their native places in China. The number of consumers relying on the farmer's income is thus extended to comprise other external relatives. We shall have more to say on the allocation of labour later on, but it may be noted in this context that only a few farmers employ workers, although some single gardeners use extra hands intermittently.

Amusements are generally few and limited to listening to the wireless set and to visits to the tea houses for the men. Every cottage has a transistor radio which besides blaring out music also provides weather forecasts and typhoon warnings. Lu Taiyun has a television set in his cottage. Surely this is a luxury for a farmer and this is the only instance we know of. Television is shown publicly also in the Tai Wai playground, and many tea shops and grocery stores (also selling soft drinks) provide television shows for their much-absorbed clientele. However, it seems that few immigrants go to watch television in these places as they are too busy in the evenings on their farms. Otherwise it may be noted

that the introduction of wireless television in Hong
Kong in 1969 caused quite a change in leisure-time
habits in this area of the New Territories. In the
evenings shops with television sets are rearranged into
small cinemas jammed with children and adults alike,
all eagerly watching the constant flow of Cantonese
opera shows.

We have stressed already that the work in the
vegetable and flower fields is continuously intense.
For the farm households the day starts between five and
six in the morning before dawn and the work continues
until one o'clock in the afternoon when people retire
to their cottages for some sleep. The rest lasts until
close on four in the afternoon when they return to the
fields. Thus they avoid the hottest hours of the day,
which, particularly during the long tropical summer,
are extremely wearing. Work now goes on until late in
the night. Often there will be only a few hours more
sleep.

It is rather difficult to get a clear picture of the
allocation of male and female work in a farming household. Certain activities seem to be performed by men
in the first place. This is true of heavy tasks
requiring physical strength, like turning the soil of a
field, manual irrigation and, but for less obvious
reasons, insecticide spraying. Harvesting often implies
heavy work and is then done by men. The cultivation and
harvesting of watercress seem to stand out as exclusively
male occupations. This may be due to the fact that these
fields require a nearly constant sprinkling of water, and
for other tasks the farmer has to squat on a sitting
board on the marshy field for many long hours. This work
is as fatiguing in hot weather as it is in cool when the
farmer wades in cold water on damp and chilly days.

Women tend to take care of flower fields where they
tend the plants and remove leaves from the stalks. They
cut grass from the dykes between the fields, harvest
crops of string beans and loofah, and do a great many
other chores in the fields. Fowl and pigs are generally
cared for by women, whereas cows are the concern of men
and women alike. Domestic tasks like cooking, washing,
and child care are in the hands of the women.

Children go to school in the daytime but help with most
household duties in their free hours. They carry water
from the village wells, sweep the cottages and give an
extra hand in the fields. They generally play with each
other on the paths around sunset.

All farmers in the Keng Hau area take one or two
breaks during their work, in the early morning, which is

mandatory, and in the afternoon, to go to a tea house in
Tin Sam or in Sha Tin Market. Weng Guiyou is an
exception. For some unknown reason he prefers to have
his tea at home.

At dawn produce for the urban markets is carried to
the collection stations. In the early morning women,
and sometimes men, set out for the local markets carrying
heavy baskets or using push-carts. Work in the fields
also starts at this time. Women return between ten and
eleven in the morning and they proceed to their domestic
tasks or to help their husbands. Children are then off
to school. Everyone returns home between noon and one
for a meal and a rest. In the late afternoon work is
resumed and continues far into the night. As has been
mentioned, insecticide spraying is done at sunset. The
cutting of flowers takes place in the late afternoon so
that they will keep better and are fresh for the market.
Flowers are tied into bundles and brought to the
collection centres from whence lorries set out for the
flower market in Boundary Street in Kowloon after midnight. The marketers – men and women alike – return
about five in the morning. Illegal vegetable marketing
is done in the late evening, legal marketing in the
early morning. We shall have more to say on this in
later chapters. Again, many farmers prefer to harvest
vegetables in the evening in order to have a fresher
produce for the market.

By and large, the allocation of work is unstructured.
There is a tendency for men to perform more heavy tasks
and for women to take care of domestic work and local
marketing.

Some farmers hire labourers to work in their fields.
Deng Fen in the Keng Hau neighbourhood usually employs
two workers. The latter are recruited from a set of
working men who apparently always work in the Sha Tin
area. They are well known among the farmers. They may
be offered jobs when working in the field, or in a tea
house. The labourers are all outsiders. Intermittently
new faces appear on this labour market, but generally
these persons need someone to act as a go-between for
them to introduce them to an employer. Sometimes
inexperienced labourers fail to satisfy the expectations
of the farmer. This has happened to Deng Fen who states
that on some occasions he has employed bad workers whom
he did not know very well. They did not know anything
about farming at all and he had to instruct them all the
time. Deng Fen pays his workmen HK\$15 a day. Their
working hours are from nine in the morning to seven in
the evening. There are no contracts and the wages are

paid out every day before the workers leave. If they wish to discontinue their employment with him they are free to do so at any time. There are no sanctions to be used against people who fail to honour mutual agreements.

Wei Chunshang of Tin Sam sometimes hires workers when time is precious. Often these labourers approach him making enquiries about jobs, and they know very well when the farmers will need them. Often he himself asks people working in neighbouring fields whether they would like to work for him when they have finished their engagement with the other farmer. Female workers he pays about seven or eight dollars a day. A man will ask for more than ten. Yue Ling in the San Tin area is alone and he needs to hire extra hands to cut his three *dou* of watercress fields. He will have to pay them "at least a few hundred dollars", which we may interpret as at least three hundred. He tries to employ labourers on a more permanent basis and therefore he pays out the wages once every month. He regards the wages as high and the reason for this is that there is a very limited number of persons available who know how to work in the fields. He says that no one would like to hire an inexperienced person. Especially for handling watercress a beginner would not dare to accept the job anyway. There are just too few really skilled farm workers in the area. He usually employs a young man surnamed Li, whose father is a farmer in Sha Tin also. Li has a city job with a water-pipe contractor, but he returns to Sha Tin every day around noon to engage in watercress cutting. Yue Ling has to pay HK$15 for his services between noon and five in the afternoon. It is much, "but of course he is very experienced."

One of the big farms of To Fung Shan has hired a man as a permanent labourer. He is a rather old man, whose main occupation is manual irrigation of those parts of the fields which are beyond reach of the sprinkler system of this technically advanced farm. We have no knowledge about his working conditions.

The existence of a small body of workers reaches far back in time. Some of the big merchants of Sha Tin Market started their careers as farmhands in the area. Ho Baixiung, a prominent businessman and politician in Sha Tin, set up a big flower and vegetable garden in the valley in the 1930s before the Pacific War and this was operated entirely by hired workers. He explains that such an enterprise would not be possible today as the costs are now so high that the farm would be run at a loss.

Ma Hua used to hire workers, but has given up this on account of the fact that it did not turn out profitably.

Although he did not actually lose money, he thought it
unwise to invest in activities not making a profit.
Instead he concentrated his farming land to a few lots
only, on which he could work himself together with his
wife. Tan Guang, who manages a big flower farm in the
surroundings of Siu Lek Yuen, is dependent on hired
labour. This is the only instance we have of an out-
sider-farmer employing villagers, that is village women.
Liu Lang from the San Tin neighbourhood used to be a farm
labourer for nearly twenty years before he started his
own farm recently.

Farm labourers are few and their wages have risen.
But few farmers can afford to hire labour. One must have
a sizeable area under cultivation in order to gain a
reasonable return if external labour is employed.
Because of the competition from the urban labour market
the number of available experienced farmhands has diminished and those who remain ask for urban wages. Most of
them seem to be relatively old men so presumably there is
a very limited recruitment of new persons to the trade.

1. Potter 1968:85.
2. Market price of land in Sha Tin in 1969 was HK$4 per square foot, whereas before the collapse of the major banks in 1964, the price was HK$5 per square foot. Few immigrants have the capital to buy land.
3. *Douzhong* should mean the area of land that is sown with one bushel of grain. As most villages had their own bushel measure the unit was most flexible in traditional times. Today it is standardized at 806.7 sq.yd. or 0.6745 hec.
4. I am obliged to the then District Officer of Tai Po District, Mr. Marriot, for his courtesy in letting me see administrative files.
5. Giles & Yung 1966, II:29f.
6. Cf. Potter 1968:83.
7. Crown Land rent is fixed at HK$3 per acre of first-class land, HK$2 per acre of second-class land, and HK$1 per acre of third-class land.
8. Potter 1968:70.
9. The process of settling in Keng Hau has been discussed further in Aijmer 1976a.
10. Further notes on the background of Sha Tin and Keng. Hau farmers are to be found in Aijmer 1973.
11. Giles & Yung 1966, I:11; II:8f.
12. For a further discussion of the implications of housing costs see Aijmer 1975.

V. CREDIT AND DEMAND

It is difficult to start farming without some money to pay for the initial expenses. Again, an inquiry into the primary investments reveals that the starting capital raised and used differs from one farmer to another. In Keng Hau, Lu Taiyun began with HK$4,000, whereas Zeng Fu in the same neighbourhood, claims that he had only three dollars in his pocket. The initial capital is accumulated by way of savings or borrowing from any likely person or institution the would-be farmer might think of, but generally loans come from relatives. Earlier, in the 1950s, it was much easier for a person to get credit from the market town shops. Farming was a prosperous trade in these years and the store-keepers were eager to cash in on the boom. This situation was drastically changed in the early sixties.

At this point we shall examine briefly the shops of Sha Tin which cater for the needs of the Countrymen.[1] There are about ten such stores in Sha Tin Market and we have made inquiries into the activities of four of these. The items they keep in stock are rice, beans, and other kinds of food, including tinned food. There are also candies and preserved fruit. Furthermore, they sell artificial fertilizers and feed for fowl. Only two shops in the town have a licence to sell insecticides. Most of these stores are managed by people who have their original homes in the Chaozhou area of northern Guangdong. The business of most market towns in the New Territories is dominated by Chaozhou men. In the Sha Tin valley, apart from the market town, Chaozhou-owned shops are to be found also in a number of villages like Sha Tin Wai, Tin Sam, and Tai Wai.

As already pointed out, vegetable farming and fowl-keeping in the New Territories experienced a boom in the 1950s when immigrants came into the area to start production and the population of the cities was increasing rapidly. These conditions were prevalent in Sha Tin as well as in other areas. As basic suppliers to the farming community, the merchants of Sha Tin tried, with considerable success, to make profit out of the new development, which brought about a rapidly progressing shift from traditional rice farming to vegetable market gardening, and the coming of the fowl farms to the valley. The store keepers extended large-scale credits without security. The boom, however, lasted but a few years.

A good many of the merchants' clients disappeared suddenly leaving behind outstanding bills. Some farmers switched rapidly from one shop to another, or availed themselves of several at the same time. Obviously the communication between the shop-owners was very limited in this respect. The keeper of one of the bigger stores maintains that he lost a sum of approximately HK$300,000 in the years 1960-63. Credit was becoming increasingly tight and the merchants developed a more cautious approach to persons soliciting trust.

To get credit today one must have been a regular customer for some time, paying for goods in cash at the time of the purchase. Only after good relations have been established in this fashion may the shop-keeper extend credit to the customer. The latter must be very prompt in settling debts, which is done ideally at Chinese New Year. No direct interest is charged, but the price of the goods delivered will be "slightly higher." This applies also to all kinds of food and other items, which the customer is expected to buy from the same shop. It is generally recognised that it is more expensive to buy goods on credit.

It happens also that the merchants provide the farmers with small money loans. We are told that they do not charge any interest on minor loans of HK$100-200. All these operations depend on the good relations between customer and store-keeper. As an example we may mention that Wei Chunshang of Tin Sam buys generally from only one store in Tai Wai where he gets what he needs on credit. It is only when he is looking for things he cannot find in his usual shop that he will try other stores in Tai Wai or in Sha Tin Market.

Apparently, then, it is cheaper for the farmer to buy the fertilizers, insecticides, seeds, and food in cash than on credit. It was often said that "we cannot afford to buy things on credit." In the Keng Hau neighbourhood we have found that people like Deng Fen, Ou, Wang, Xie, and Huang, who insist that they pay cash for the goods they need from the shops, do not go regularly to one specific store to buy. They are flexible and have a free choice. Independent of credit facilities they can use all possible advantages provided by the market-town shops. Also Lu Taiyun makes a point in paying cash, still he favours only one merchant, presumably because of his long-standing relations with this man.

People who are dependent on getting goods on credit, like Chen Quan, Deng Shoufu, and Weng Guiyou, generally use two shops. This may be due partly to the fact that only two shops in Sha Tin are licensed to sell

insecticides. But is is also possible that the credit-
seeker builds up a strategic position from which he can
exploit two merchants at the same time. Two credit books
diminish the undertakings of each creditor. But sometimes even two stores are insufficient and the merchant
comes into a position where he can exploit the farmer.
The remarkable fact that Chen Quan has to accept fertilizers from one shop, although this Keng Hau farmer thinks
that they are mixed with other stuffs to the degree that
they are even harmful to the soil, and at a higher price
than he usually pays, is explained by his credit book in
that shop. This merchant knows that Chen has to put up
with what he has to offer. Under these circumstances it
is natural that Chen tries to do the best part of his
business with his main shop - that of Liu Rensheng in
Sha Tin Market. It is only when he does not want to
strain his relations with Liu that he will try the other
place.

Employees of the merchants deliver the commodities to
the farm, and they seek out the customers in the field to
make inquiries about and solicit their purchases. Thus a
person can order things whenever he meets a *fuji* of a
store he frequents. The use of such services tends to
limit the existing choices, as a person has to be reasonably well acquainted with the employees of the stores to
trust that his orders will be attended to.

Thus the market-town shops form one of the most
important sources for the farmer to obtain credit for
his enterprise. By and large, most well-established
farmers can have access to seeds, fertilizers, and insecticides on credit, if they think that this will be to
their advantage. A few will also have the opportunity to
receive small loans from the shop keepers. What other
means to get economic assistance exist in Sha Tin and how
are they used?

In the first place, people may borrow money from
friends and relatives. It has been difficult to secure
more systematic information on this. But we have seen in
an earlier context that Chen Quan financed his house-
building project in Keng Hau by way of borrowing money
from his wife's relatives in Hong Kong, and also from his
close neighbour Lu Taiyun. Liu Chenzhi, a villager from
Sha Tin Tau, explained that "farmers could ask assistance
from friends and relatives, but the sum would generally
be very small. People who are friends and relatives of
the farmer will also be poor and it would not be
possible for them to offer assistance for new investments." Ma Hua, a Chaozhou farmer of Pak Tin, explains
that one reason why he does not like the idea of moving

away from the area he lives in, is that he has very
good relations with his neighbours. In case of exigency
he could always obtain some money and assistance from
his friends there. Lu Taiyun of Keng Hau, Chen's bene-
factor, expressed the view that "you can borrow from
friends at any moment, even one thousand dollars. You
just say you need the money and you get it."

Certainly only prosperous friends can afford to have
outstanding loans of one thousand dollars. And surely
the person who borrows must be a man of some means too
and have a trustworthy and profitable farming enterprise. When Lu lent money to Chen this was due to the
mutual obligation of a long-standing relationship. We
do not know how much money was involved, nor the terms
of the loan, but as an expression of friendship it is
not likely to involve interest nor to be refundable
within a specified time limit. By and large, we suspect
that the passing of loans between friends and neighbours is not frequent, and if this occurs the sums are
comparatively small. That kinship may be an effective
channel for loans is demonstrated by the case of Chen
Quan. However, it should be noted that his affinal
relatives do not live in Sha Tin, but are urban
residents on Hong Kong Island.

One instance of borrowing from a more professional
money lender is revealed in a District Office dossier:

> I Chen Gongxiu, native of Sha Tin Tau village, beg
> respectfully to submit that I received a loan of
> HK$7,000 from a Mr. Zeng for the sake of my serious
> disease which I contracted last year. The agree-
> ment was made for a period of 1 year - 6/9/58-
> 5/9/59 at an interest of HK$30 per HK$1,000 per
> month with my houses and farm land as mortgage . . .
> being a farmer . . . I could not afford to pay HK$210
> per month . . . (I had) to sell my houses or farm
> lands separately in order to repay by installments
> . . . sold house for HK$4,000 . . . pig shed HK$1,500
> and handed over the lump sum of HK$5,500 to the
> lender as soon as I received the money.[2]

Another possibility of obtaining a loan is from a
marketing middleman with whom the farmer has co-operated
for some time. We shall have more to say about these
agents in Chapter VII. Suffice it here to note that for
instance Liu Lang, living near San Tin, says that one
advantage of having close connexions with one particular
middleman is that you might borrow money from him. We
have similar hints from other informants; still, we do

not think of middlemen as important sources for loans.
Most informants declaim their money-lending function.
Nor do we think that landlords lend money to their
tenants as the contacts between the two generally seem
very limited. However, landlords may allow tenants to
postpone the payment of rent. We do not know of any
pawnshops or professional money-brokers in the market-
towns or in the villages. The case described above
shows that expensive credit is available from some
villagers. The activities of these men are directed
towards business and politics, and money-lending is
just a sideline. Immigrant farmers cannot afford the
high interests, nor do they as tenants without house
and land have the necessary security.

Likewise, we have not found any evidence for the
existence of revolving loan societies.[3] Such groups
of people are common in the New Territories and one
example in Sha Tin is the Sha Tin Chamber of Commerce
which, among other functions, operates a revolving loan-
society for the benefit of the shop owners of Sha Tin
Market. The organizing of a loan-society requires a
participation of a number of persons in order to
operate. As I hope to show elsewhere, the immigrant
vegetable farmer's network of social relations will
hardly be extensive enough to secure a reasonable
recruitment of interested persons, a fact which may
well explain their absence. We have no information on
the village population in this respect; we guess that
in the absence of a large number of men - now living
abroad or in the cities - such loan-societies are
mainly in the hands of women. Certainly, they do not
normally benefit the capital raising of a village
farmer.

The Hong Kong Government, through its Department
of Agriculture and Fisheries (in 1969), extends credit
facilities from a number of funds to the rural population of the New Territories. These are mainly the
Kadoorie Agricultural Aid Loan Fund, started in 1955
by the Government and Messrs. Laurence and Horace
Kadoorie, Hong Kong industrialists. The fund is
administered by the department whose director is chairman and trustee. Loans are also available through the
J.E. Joseph Trust Fund and through the Vegetable
Marketing Organization Loan Fund. The Kadoorie Agricultural Aid Association, a philanthropic organization
also founded by the Kadoorie brothers, aims at giving
grants to members of the farming community who cannot
find enough capital on their own. The latter is a
private organization but it operates in close contact

with the Department of Agriculture. However, this vast
repository of money is only rarely tapped by the
farmers of the Sha Tin valley. The governmental wealth
is conducted down to the local level through a number
of agencies. The Sha Tin Rural Committee is important
in this respect. The Rural Committee is a body of
elected or nominated Village Representatives, run by an
Executive Committee and housed with meeting and office
facilities in premises close by Sha Tin Market. The
office there is an important centre for people of
influence in the area, for Village Representatives on
official business, or for people generally who want to
obtain legal information, register births and deaths,
or just complain. The Rural Committee office is also
a place where applications for loans from official
sources are handled.

The farmer completes an application form and leaves
this with the Committee. The Department of Agriculture
has an officer stationed in the Committee building, who
collects these applications. This man investigates the
circumstances pertaining to each case. This done he
forwards the documents to more high-level decision
makers. If the outcome is a positive one the farmer
may collect the money at the Rural Committee office.
However, there is a general trend among the farmers to
distrust these facilities. For instance, Liu Chenzhi,
a villager of Sha Tin Tau, explains the procedure in
the following terms: "Theoretically the Department
should supply money-loans to the farmers. However, in
practice it is very complicated. First one has to
forward an application for the loan. Next there will
be an officer coming to investigate the living conditions of your family. He wants to know how many
persons there are in the family and how many of them
have jobs. He also wants to know the size of your
land and the approximate value of the crops on that
land. He takes notes of the monthly expenditures for
your livelihood and of your expenses for the education
of your children. Furthermore he wants an estimate of
the value of each single crop grown. The further
investigation in the Department will take at least six
months, and if the farmer in the end gets any money at
all, it is much too late."

Two factors account, we think, for the fact that
people generally avoid borrowing money from official
sources. The farmer feels uneasy in a situation of
straightforward interrogation. He is, as we have
noted above, inclined to deal with economic matters in
an informal way, and to him, documents, a technical

procedure, and formal treatment are signs of distrust
on behalf of the other party. Again, the bureaucratic
procedure is to him a disguise of more normal ways of
handling money. Xiung Ko, a Dongguan watercress farmer
in the Kak Tin neighbourhood, explains that he and his
brother "made inquiries about a loan from the Department of Agriculture, but they were not successful. As
they do not know anyone working there they were in fact
just wasting time." The other factor is the long
waiting time. We do not know how much time the procedure actually requires, but what matters here is the
farmer's belief that it will take some six months, and
this notion determines how he will act.

In the Rural Committee it was explained to us that
the vegetable farmers do not have to come to the
Committee office as they have their own associations.
"If they want to borrow money they could approach the
chairman of their association and he will assist them
with the application." We shall here look into these
possibilities. The Co-operative Society of Sha Tin
is supposed to connect farmers with governmental
funds as well as the Vegetable Marketing Organization.
Co-operatives in the New Territories have frequently
been described as successful instruments for the benefit
of the farming community.[4] Unfortunately, the Sha Tin
Co-operative Society cannot match such claims. The
management was never particularly efficient and it was
just about non-existent during the troubled year of
1967 and thereafter.

The latter development was one aspect of the
political struggle, and politics account also for the
fact that many farmers avoid this organization. However, it is not only right-wingers or 'neutralists' who
shun the Co-operative; also most communists are very
hesitant. In fact, most farmers deny that they can
obtain credit through the Co-operative Society. Thus
it seems as if comparatively few persons take advantage
of this channel to the governmental founts. It is quite
possible that the executive of the Co-operative handles
only the applications from the farmers who are 'card
carrying members.' There were in 1969 26 members of the
Co-operative Society. If the assumption above is
correct, then the capacity of the Co-operative to handle
credit for the farming community of Sha Tin is extremely
limited.

There are two other somewhat different co-operatives
in Sha Tin. They are the Tai Ling Pig Breeders' Credit
Association and the Pak Tin Pig Breeders' Credit

Association. We have no useful information on the former of these two societies, but is is reasonable to believe that they are fairly similar. The Pak Tin association is formally for pig breeders, but the main occupation of four of the members, with whom we are acquainted, is gardening. These men are all very concerned about the technical development of their enterprises. We have mentioned earlier such features as electric light over the flower fields and automatic sprinkler irrigation. They have all well-built houses. The technical installations represent expensive equipment, and it is the close co-operation of this society with the Department of Agriculture which has brought about the financing of these costly projects. Naturally, the Association operates only for the benefit of its member households, who seem to be twelve in number. It will act as a guarantor for loans from different funds administered by the Department. We are under the general impression that the Tai Ling association is rather less successful in this respect.

However, there is another way to approach the governmental wealth. The China Light and Power Co. has an office in Sha Tin and one member of the staff there also acts as an agent for the Department of Agriculture. He is generally referred to as "the Englishman in the electric light company." That the China Light and Power Co. fulfils this function is due to the fact that it is under the directorship of the Kadoorie brothers who, as already mentioned, have taken a keen interest in the welfare of the New Territories' farmers. This channel is considered less troublesome and is the one the farmers in the Keng Hau area have in mind if they need extra money.

In fact, it was even suggested that one could use such credit for speculative purposes. As Wei Fa put it: "If the amount is under one thousand dollars there is no interest. If it is more there is an interest of seven per cent. You have to pay it back in six months' time. In fact, you can borrow money from this officer and then deposit the sum in the bank. By way of this procedure you can make a profit out of the bank interest." We do not know whether such manipulations have ever taken place or whether this is just a general speculation about the possibility for this kind of activity. But other people are less sophisticated. Chen Quan, for instance, said that he "suspects that the Englishman has something to do with Government." Such vague knowledge will hardly invite manipulation.

We may speculate on why 'the Englishman' is preferred to the Co-operative Society or the Rural Committee. We believe that the mere designation 'the Englishman' says something to the effect that the farmer feels that in that office he deals with someone who has a direct contact with the sphere of influence. An Englishman in an office must be more powerful than a Chinese in the same position. We may also note that the Rural Committee is not a place where an immigrant farmer feels comfortable, whereas the China Light office is a neutral place where the farmer's social persona is irrelevant and therefore not inferior. This argument is necessarily vague and impressionistic as we have not observed the interaction of such loan negotiations in these offices.

Loans from governmental sources are supplemented by stipends and grants from the Community Relief Trust Fund in times of distress caused by natural calamities. Loans and subsidies are often combined. This may be best illustrated by two examples. Ma Hua, on the slopes of the Pak Tin valley, had the experience that his farm was damaged badly by the typhoon 'Wanda' in 1962. On this occasion he obtained 'compensation' from the Government amounting to HK$800, but he had to pay back half of the sum 'in due course'. In fact, when he received the money he immediately returned HK$400, and spent the rest buying pigs.

Governmental allowances for help in difficult situations do not exceed HK$100 normally. Such grants were paid out on the occasion of the heavy rainstorm in the summer of 1969, when the whole valley was flooded. The fact that money could be obtained was spread by rumour in an entirely informal way. Chen Quan was one of those in Keng Hau who picked up this bit of information. He walked to the Sha Tin Rural Committee where he completed some forms. He hoped that he would be 'compensated' by some 50-60 dollars. It is interesting to note that the farmer's talk about 'compensation' seems to imply a notion that the Hong Kong Government is in some way responsible for weather conditions in the Colony.

We should note also that money can be borrowed from the marketing organization of Tai Wai. We know of only one farmer who makes use of this market, and he is of the opinion that the procedure there is much too troublesome as a person who wishes to borrow money will need four guarantors to vouch for him. We do not possess any further knowledge about this credit facility.

The Sha Tin vegetable and flower grower is exposed to risks. In Chapter II we have given an outline of the

hazardous conditions created by capricious weather and
unstable market prices. So far we have tried to
describe the means available to the farmer for his
accommodation to the unstable reality of Sha Tin. The
distribution of success is quite uneven. We have
suggested already that the more prosperous gardeners,
who live a life in relative comfort even by urban
standards, are those who have a more 'commercial' background and are more knowledgeable in the spheres of
management and economics. Even the life of a less
successful farmer has a lot of attraction when compared
to that of an urban wage earner[5] - and this is often
emphasized - in that not working for others he is "free
to do whatever he likes". Of course, the need to subsist limits his freedom in a drastic way, but nevertheless the image of freedom persists both as a means to
give dignity to one's occupation and to conceal the fact
that unskilled and illiterate people have very few
chances in the urban areas.

But the lure of the cities is present. No one wants
his children to continue the farming. However, few
gardeners seem to give up. In the autumn of 1967 Xiung
Ko, his brother, and a 'village brother' had just set
up a watercress farm near Kak Tin as a joint venture.
Their expectations were not fulfilled, and in early
winter the 'village brother' was forced to leave the
farm as three persons could not make a living out of
the land. Again, in summer 1969 on my return to Sha
Tin, all of them were gone and no one knew where. In
the Keng Hau neighbourhood the gardeners are well
settled. However, the cottage now inhabited by Cheng
Zhiming was one occupied by a man surnamed Wang who
gave up his farming life and moved to Tai Wai where he
now runs a grocery store specializing in tinned food
and soft drinks. Another man surnamed Li used to live
in one of the Keng Hau huts, but is said to have
returned to his native village in China. Whether this
is only temporarily so, no one seems to know.

We have stressed already that the fluctuations of
the market price are important for the understanding of
the hazardousness of the garden production. The main
factor affecting the market price in Hong Kong is the
import of food from the People's Republic of China, but
also, on a much smaller scale, from Taiwan, Japan, and
Southeast Asia. Large barges loaded with fresh
vegetables from the Canton hinterland come in daily to
the vegetable market of Kennedy Town on Hong Kong
Island, and freighters come down imtermittently from
north China ports with northern produce. These import

goods amount to about 50 per cent of the Hong Kong consumption. Low prices accompany these products and the New Territories farmer's individual enterprise has to compete with a large-scale production handled by labour brigades of People's Communes.[6]

Granted seasonal variations, we must assume that the Hong Kong consumers cause a fairly even market demand as vegetables form a major part of the daily food. However, the supply from China is uneven, due to the conditions for production and political decisions there. This means that the demands of the consumers are not always satisfied by Chinese products and in that case the prices tend to mount rapidly. It is by exploiting these lacunae that the local farmers can get their best returns. With respect to which kind of vegetable lacunae will emerge, it is impossible to predict, so a general rational strategy for the planning and planting of crops cannot be resorted to; resorting to gardening indicates a strong element of gambling.

Also, it should be noted that there has been a steadily increasing number of farmers in the New Territories since the early 1950s. More and more people have become competitors on the vegetable market at the same time as the imports from China and elsewhere have been on the increase. According to the vegetable farmers of Sha Tin, who have been established there in gardening for a considerable time, their economic situation was formerly much more favourable. As Lu Taiyun in Keng Hau sums up: "At first the conditions were much better than they are now. There were only a few outsiders in this area at that time and most of the local villagers grew rice. It was only me and the other outsiders who preferred to grow vegetables. Eventually the local villagers followed us and switched over to vegetables, and the number of outsiders increased. Consequently life was getting more difficult."

The farmers who specialize in flowers do not have to engage in similar competition. Instead the fluctuations in prices are caused by fluctuations in demand. Prices rise at the time of the festivals of the calendar, culminating in the Chinese New Year. Also Western feasts, increasingly popular and celebrated in Hong Kong, cause a rise in prices to the benefit of the gardener. Quite naturally, the political events of 1967 on the Hong Kong scene brought hardship to the flower cultivators as people in the cities lost interest in flowers in the midst of violent riots and intense terror-bombing. However, what was bad for the flower gardeners was to the advantage of the vegetable growers as Chinese supplies were running short for several months and consequently market prices soared.

   Also flower growers have increased in number owing to the arrival of new immigrants and the fact that native villagers have become engaged in this use of land. On the eastern side of Tide Cove most of the land is planted with flowers, and a number of villagers from places like Siu Lek Yuen and Ngau Pei Sha have taken part in this development.

NOTES TO CHAPTER V

1. These shops have other functions as well, to which I
   hope to return in a different context.
2. File T.P. 13/164/59, to be seen at the Tai Po
   District Office, New Territories, Hong Kong.
3. These have been described repeatedly in the literature, see e.g. Fei 1939:267-74, Feng & Yung 1931,
   Gamble 1954:260-70, Smith 1899:152-60, and Wu
   1936:176.
4. See e.g. Cater 1954:4f, and K. Topley 1962:4.
5. In 1969 the wages for workmen in Hongkong and
   Kowloon rarely exceeded HK$500; e.g. shop workers of
   higher-class stores earn HK$300-350 per month at
   this time. (Baird 1970:8). In 1966 it was estimated
   that the average cost of living per person per month
   was HK$102.8, which figure should be compared with the
   corresponding Sha Tin average of HK$68.6, according to
   the earlier mentioned social survey of the same year.
   Wah Kiu Yat Po, May 1st, 1966; Giles & Yung 1966, II:9.
6. There have been rumours that the Hong Kong import of
   vegetables should have provided the incentive for the
   organization of farms near the border, specialized in
   market gardening for Hong Kong consumption, but we
   have no evidence at all to support this assumption.
   See e.g. *South China Morning Post,* August 22nd 1963.

VI. SOME OTHER ACTIVITIES

To make the picture of farming activities in Sha Tin more complete we should mention some other types of cultivation which take place besides the growing of rice, vegetables and flowers. In the Tai Ling area there are some fields planted with sugar cane and near Che Kung Miu on an islet in the Shing Mun River there is a dense plantation of banana trees. On the northern side of the Kowloon Hills a large area has been planted with tung oil trees. On the hillsides there are also orchards with lychee and dragon-eye trees. Some of these orchards are quite extensive and belong to the old villages; the largest of them all is owned and managed by a man from San Tin.

Immigrants own smaller orchards. One example is Chen Han, a man of Shunde origin, who has some vegetable fields in the Yue Yuen area but who also spends much of his time on his hillside fruit orchard. He has some peach and mandarin trees there and also pineapples. The former are grown in pots for the flower markets at Chinese New Year. Liu Lang, who is a watercress farmer near the village of San Tin is a joint owner of a small orchard. This, however, is situated on the other side of the New Territories on the very coastline of Deep Bay near Ha Tsuen. The journey from San Tin to this orchard takes two or three hours. Around Sha Tin Market there are several gardens for potted flowers, trees as well as miniature trees. Such enterprises occur intermittently all over the valley. There is, for instance, one near San Tin, apart from the big orchard and garden of the Buddhist nunnery there. In Tai Ling and Tung Lou Wan there are some old bamboo groves. We have not made any detailed inquiries into the activities pertaining to these types of cultivation, nor do we know anything about the sugar-cane plantation near Pak Shek.

Again, we should add a few remarks on animal husbandry. We have mentioned already cows and buffaloes and their use as draught animals for ploughing. Of course they are also kept for their meat as their fodder is inexpensive. Mostly they are allowed to grass on the hillsides, along the paths, and on abandoned fields. Immigrants do not have buffaloes. The small hunch-backed cows are sold off to the abattoir in Pak Tin. In the customary Chinese way, no one cares for the milk. In Keng Hau, Ou Xi has got one cow and two calves, which means that he intends them for the meat market. The raising of cows does not add substantially to the household economy, but the manure is important as a fertilizer for the fields.

Sometimes pigs are raised on a larger scale. There
is a pig farm in Yue Yuen, which is quite big, and, for
instance, Ma Hua in Pak Tin depends on his pig breeding
for the livelihood of his family. Again, competition
from China imports has affected the importance of pig
breeding heavily. The same applies to cow rearing, but
hogs are much more expensive to feed and therefore
larger investments are required. The keeping of pig
pens is a true business activity. In the early fifties
pork fetched quite high prices on the market. For
sucking-pig one could get as much as HK$600 per picul
and for ordinary quality of meat over HK$200.[1] But
imports have affected the prices and every day special
trains loaded with masses of pigs are brought in from
Guangdong to the Yau Ma Tei railway station in Kowloon,
from whence they are sent to the slaughter houses.
Thus prices are much lower nowadays and the breeder's
margins are narrow indeed.

Farmers who have spacious pig pens and who used to
have a large number of animals, have today only a few
left. They do not get much profit from them but can
use their droppings for the fertilization of their
vegetable fields. Chen Quan of Keng Hau used to have
a few pigs up to a few years ago when he gave up
altogether owing to the low market price, and planted
the land occupied by the pens with flowers. However,
he would like to make another attempt but cannot now
raise the capital for the initial expenses. Possibly
he is also kept back by his wife. His idea is that one
can feed the pigs with waste from the farming and such
produce as one cannot sell in the market. This would
decrease the expenditure for the feeding. He would
also get fertilizers.

Ou Xi, also in the Keng Hau neighbourhood, gave up
pig breeding in 1966 owing to the falling market prices.
The native population had the same experience. There
are still pigs kept in the villages but in our experience it is never an important feature of the economy.
Rather, the hogs provide some working tasks for old
people who drive them along the paths and on the lower
hill slopes. It should be mentioned also that squatters
who are not farmers sometimes keep one or two hogs in a
small backyard. This can be seen in the large squatter
areas around Sha Tin Tau, for instance.

Ma Hua in Pak Tin still clings to his pig business.
He is of the opinion that there is still a small profit
to be made from this activity. He has established
contact with a restaurant in Sha Tin Market and he
receives their waste at a cost of HK$40 a month. If he

were dependent on buying pig feed in a regular way the
breeding business would not be profitable - rather the
contrary. The sociological survey of Sha Tin of 1966
lists 12 families - out of a sample of 86 - raising 283
pigs, giving a total yearly income of HK$43,790. One
animal should thus be worth some 150 dollars and each
pig-raising family - granted an even distribution of
the animals - an annual income of HK$3,641.[2]

The raising of poultry has undergone a similar change.
From about 1949 there was a sudden appearance of in-
numerable new poultry farms, especially in the Ping Shan
area of the New Territories. Part of this boom was due
to investments of Shanghai capital. But already in 1951
farmers learned about low prices.[3] Extensive breeding
is still found scattered over the Sha Tin area, notably
on the slopes of To Fung Shan, in Tung Lo Wan, and Tin
Sam. Most farmers have a few hens and sometimes ducks
for their own consumption. The fowl stroll freely around
the farmer's cottage or are kept in huge bamboo baskets.

Ma Hua - the Pak Tin man - earlier became engaged in
the raising of poultry for the market; 500 birds were
intended for the Chongyang festival and 500 for the
Chinese New Year. The venture ended in a complete failure and he lost some HK$3,000. He explains that for a
poor family that sum is equal to their expenditures for
a whole year. To recover the 3,000 dollars the whole
family had to work very hard for many years, as it is
difficult to save so large a sum. The main reason for
the failure was the Chinese export of poultry to Hong
Kong. Ma Hua explains: "There is one main reason why
no one is interested in poultry farming. Already at the
end of the hatching procedure, when the egg has become
a small chicken, the costs amount to two dollars a
piece. Then one has to add all the feed and the cost
will be several times higher before the hen is ready for
the market. But a China hen will generally cost three
dollars."

Keng Hau people can observe the poultry farm in the
Tin Sam area, which is run by a villager surnamed Lo from
nearby Lo Uk Tsuen, and also the farm at Che Kung Miu,
on their expeditions to Sha Tin Market. Apparently these
do not incite them to try large-scale poultry farming
themselves. Two of them have experience. Lu Taiyun
made an attempt in 1961 but gave up as, allegedly, it
took too much time. Huang Fanwu's household used to
raise 250 chickens but they contracted an epidemic
disease and they all died. However, they still maintain
a small poultry farm where they have some one hundred
fowl. They say they do not dare to have more. It is a

rather primitive farm and the incomes are only supplementary to those of other activities. In the 1966 Sha Tin survey 80 out of 136 'village families' raised poultry, but only four for cash. However, only three of these four families reported a profit from poultry in 1965.[4]

There were a few dovecots in the Che Kung Miu area, but in 1969 only one was still in existence; the others had by then been taken over by people busy breaking old plastic toys into tiny fragments. We may also note that the former reclaimed rice-land inside the islet of Yuen Chow Kok, which was submerged after typhoon damage on the protecting sea walls, is now used for fish ponds. Again, the 1966 survey found two families busy with fish husbandry in a sample of 86 squatter households. The total yearly income of these two families is given as HK$70,000.[5]

We have mentioned already that textile factories are the major industrial enterprise in the valley. There is also a great deal of cottage industry, such as bean-curd processing, plaiting of plastic 'rattan ware,' manufacturing of handbags, plastic flower assembling, and other similar occupations. A traditional feature is the manufacturing of joss-sticks in the village of Sha Tin Tau.[6] Most of these tasks are carried out in the villages and compact squatter areas, and to a large extent by women - wives of wage-earning men - who do such manufacturing as a sideline to the household chores, while they simultaneously take care of the children.

We should mention also the keeping of small tea and mahjong shops and stores - particularly in Hung Mui Kuk - mainly for the invasion of Sunday tourists. There are also the more pretentious restaurants, including a fancifully decorated floating restaurant, which provides superb Cantonese (and sometimes Hakka and even Sichuanese) food for well-to-do townspeople. Small food stalls are everywhere in the market-town and in the nearby surroundings. There are ugly areas which look like scrap yards, but what they are really used for is beyond our knowledge. This brief account does less than justice to the multitude of odd activities going on in the suburbanized Sha Tin. Outwardly they are reflected in a rapidly increasing ugliness devastating the once famous rustic scenery.

We must consider yet another feature of the farming household economy, which has been mentioned in passing already. Among the Keng Hau immigrant farmers, nine households have members who are wage earners and who contribute to some degree to the support of the household group. As usual, we are not well informed as to the amounts or what percentage of the household budget such external income

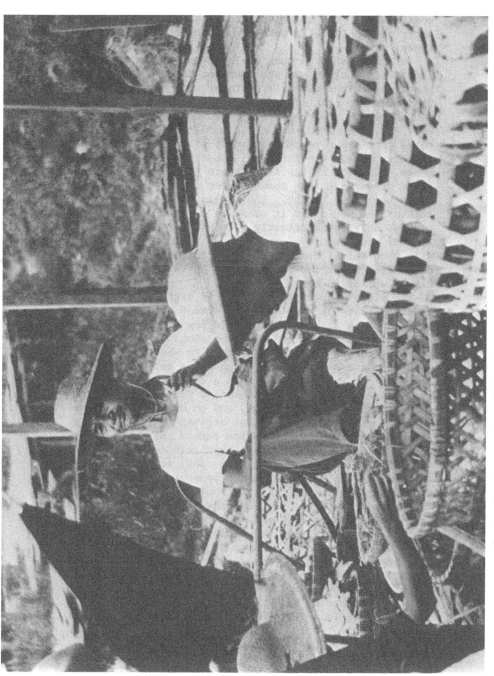

3. Lo Cai (centre) waiting for customers in Sha Tin Market

constitutes. The field situation has not allowed the entry of such details into the anthropologist's note-books.

We know that Chen Quan's eldest daughter works in a factory in Kowloon and she commutes from Sha Tin where she lives in her father's cottage. The household of Zhao Huosheng consists of his family and a man surnamed Li, who works in a textile factory in town. We do not know how integrated they are economically. Wang Bei works in a paper company in town, while his wife and daughter manage the farm. His wages are HK$400 a month. His son-in-law lives there also; he is a super-visor of workers in a construction company and his wages amount to HK$500. The son-in-law does not par-take of the meals and it seems as if he sleeps in the cottage only intermittently. In another household Wu Xian is a worker in a gas plant in Kowloon while his wife Chen Meigui manages the farm together with their daughter. Their son-in-law lives there also; he is a bakery worker in town.

The eldest daughter of Lo Cai is sixteen years old. We guess that she must have employment outside Sha Tin. In Deng Shouhua's household the oldest son is working as an apprentice in a workshop, to which he has been introduced by Wu An's brother Fu who is employed by the same company. Deng's son has a salary of HK$150 a month. Wu Fu, then, works in a company selling and repairing typewriters in Hongkong's Central District. Saturday afternoons, Sundays, and on holidays he helps in the farm. When Wu An first arrived in the Keng Hau area he was himself a part-time farmer only with a low-pay job with the Department of Agriculture and Fish-eries in Kowloon during the day. This is not an unusual way for an immigrant to launch a farming enter-prise. Ma Hua in Pak Tin, for instance, left his wife to take charge of the land and the pigs when they moved into their present location. He continued his job as a wharf coolie until they were able to save enough money for a large investment in more pigs. Eventually he quit the coolie job and concentrated on his farm.

In Keng Hau the eldest son of the Weng family has got a job in town. He seldom comes back and it is doubtful whether he still can be regarded as a member of the household. The Huang family's two eldest sons are working in town. One is a mechanic in a motor car workshop, the other is a 'cloth cutter' in a textile factory. The degree to which such external incomes are pooled with the income from the farm certainly varies a great deal owing to the wage earner's position, age and sex. We may assume that Chen Quan's daughter gives up most of her income whereas Wu An's brother certainly uses up the best part of his wages in the company of his peers.

In the Sha Tin valley, paddy fields were still in 1969 to be seen scattered around in the area. Here we shall not deal with the techniques and activities pertaining to traditional rice cultivation as there are ample descriptions elsewhere.[7] The New Territories are situated in the double-cropping area of Guangdong, and two crops of rice are still harvested in the mountain villages high above the Sha Tin valley. In the lowland this has changed and generally only one crop is harvested there. This is planted during the summer months. However, there are still a few stubborn villagers who go in for the two traditional rice crops. The grain is nowadays for the farmer's own consumption.[8]

1. Retail price for pork of standard quality was in 1969 around HK$330 per picul. In 1958 one catty was worth around HK$450 on the market. See *Cost of Living Survey 1968 - 63/64*, p.26.
2. Giles & Yung 1966, I:17.
3. Keen 1950:3 Barrow 1951:6, and 1952:8.
4. Giles & Yung 1966, I:17.
5. Giles & Yung 1966, I:17.
6. Cf. Chang 1963. However, it is hardly justified to believe that this is a remainder of the supposedly famous industry in Sha Tin, and Sha Tin Tau is anyway a fairly recent village.
7. Blackie 1955, Francke 1913, Gibbs 1931, Grant 1960, Groves and Walker 1967, King 1926, and Wagner 1926 are a few examples of such descriptions.
8. The exchange system for rice, when high quality local produce was traded directly for larger amounts of imported low-quality grain from Thailand and Burma, formerly quite important in the New Territories, now seems to be on the decline. Maybe this is a reflection of the higher standard of living.

VII. MARKETING

Sha Tin Market is a new township in the New Territories.
Some minor commerce has always been carried out in the
close vicinity of the railway station from small stalls
and by hawkers. The market place here developed spontaneously in the post-Pacific War period at the same
time as Sha Tin became increasingly popular as a week-
end resort for urbanites, a feature which, in its turn,
attracted more hawkers. Governmental initiatives were
taken in the early 1950s to bring order to this development:

> At Shatin, a place which since the war has attracted
> great crowds from Kowloon at week-ends, the hawker
> problem was becoming unmanageable. It was solved by
> getting the owner of the marshy land opposite the
> station to fill it and build a planned lay-out,
> including roads, public latrine, and water supply.[1]

And a year after, it was reported that

> A new market was built by the Sha Tin Rural Committee
> on Crown Land at Sha Tin. It will be run by the
> Committee.[2]

Although the township has a very regular layout it
has acquired a rather traditional market-town flavour
comparable with what one finds elsewhere in the New
Territories' old centres of trade. Brilliant boards
and posters advertise the goods and services available
in the different shops. Tea houses and restaurants are
abundant. The display of merchandise emerges from the
open-fronted shops to fill up a good proportion of the
otherwise unusually wide streets. Pedlars of foods and
delicacies push their way through the throngs of people
who fill the market during the morning hours. The tea
shops are very busy in the mornings, the restaurants
liven up around lunchtime and in the evenings, and when
dusk falls the many sea-food and fried bean-curd booths
come out into the streets. There are shops for all
kinds of daily commodities and fresh food is sold in an
open market hall in the centre of the town, where
permanent stalls retail to the customers of the Sha Tin
valley.
During the last few years the market has expanded in
a rather unorderly manner in a westerly direction from
the main lay-out. But here one also finds one of the

earliest spontaneous additions to the permanently
planned town arrangement. This is the row of hawkers
who squat along the sea front path along the embank-
ment of Tide Cove. Here Hoklo fishermen trade their
nightly catch, fowl breeders spread out their huge
bamboo containers with live ducks and poultry, and
vegetable farmers line up with their push-carts and
baskets of fresh garden produce.

This is the place and the setting for the most
frequent marketing operations of the Keng Hau farmers -
although it may not be so for vegetable growers in
other areas of Sha Tin. Still, this market seems to
have a place in the lives of most inhabitants of the
valley. The only other alternative of some importance
is the village town of Tai Wai where there is an
authorized minor market in an open square, run by the
Village Council. Only one farmer of Keng Hau takes
advantage of the facilities there.

In the early morning low four-wheeled push-carts are
loaded with vegetable baskets and brought to Sha Tin
Market along the winding and narrow paths on the dykes
between the fields. So far as we know all vegetables sold
there are of local origin. In the market town two
choices are offered to the producer. On one hand he
can sell his greens to one of the dealers who manage
permanent stalls in the authorized food market of the
town; these persons, in their turn, will retail the
vegetables to the consumers. On the other hand, the
farmer may choose to sell his produce himself to the
consumers by way of hawking on the sea-front path.
Let us consider some further data on the marketing
procedure of the Keng Hau farmers.

Ou Xi always aims at selling his vegetables himself,
as does Chen Quan, but generally his wife takes care of
the marketing, both selling to the stalls and hawking
on the path. Zhao Huosheng sends his wife to the
market where she, in the first place, does the hawking,
but sometimes she sells to the stalls also. Again, the
Wang household takes advantage of both these opportunities. Zeng Chengda says he prefers to sell the
vegetables he grows by hawking them himself in Sha Tin
Market, but occasionally he takes advantage of the stall-
businessmen. The same applies to Chen Meigui. Wang Di,
the wife of Xie Xien, sells her produce herself.

Generally Lu Taiyun sells his vegetables in Tai Wai.
This successful farmer has a market stall of his own in
the private market of that big village. He is also the
licensee of a booth in Sha Tin but it is only seldom he

will use this one as his first choice is the Tai Wai
market where his wife sells every day. For the stall
in Tai Wai he has to pay a fee of HK$50 a month whereas
the Sha Tin Market booth is only HK$10 a year. We may
mention also that we have seen Lo Cai sit by the path
at Sha Tin Market waiting for customers but we have not
been able to discuss these matters with him. Wu An
claims that he sells his vegetables to the stall
merchants in Sha Tin Market. His old father takes care
of bringing the produce there and selling it to the
dealers. The wife of the Huang domestic group hawks in
Sha Tin Market the vegetables they grow.

There is consensus of opinion as to the determinants
for the choice between the alternative ways to sell
produce. If a farm yields only small amounts of vegetables ripe for the market, the general strategy
employed seems to be hawking. It is only when the crops
are plentiful that the stalls are seriously considered.
A lot of produce may be difficult for a single person to
handle, and the obvious arrangement under these circumstances is an agreement with a stall dealer. Of course,
this implies the acceptance of a lower price. As Zhao
Huosheng put it: "When we get too much we sell it to the
stalls. However, the price offered by the stall is too
low. If the market price is one dollar for a catty, the
stall manager will only pay you 60-70 cents." But the
advantage is there. The merchant buys the whole quantity
and pays cash. The procedure is quick, the reward
immediate, and valuable time and effort saved.

The latter circumstances may be considered by some
producers a point of so much importance that they supply
the market retail dealers all the time. In any case,
there is a choice between a number of different dealers,
and all informants agree that it is the price offered
which determines to whom you sell. The highest price
paid gets the deal. We have not been able to trace any
more stable connexions between certain producers/
suppliers and certain stall merchants. We cannot rule
out their existence entirely but we have no data at all
to hint at such specific commercial relations.

We have mentioned that Lu Taiyun has two stalls -
one in Tai Wai and one in Sha Tin Market. In his use of
these two facilities he employs a rather similar
strategy in that normal yields are brought to Tai Wai
by his wife every day to be sold in the retail market
there. When production is high the stall in Sha Tin
Market comes in handy and then the surplus is sold
there. To manage one's own stall entails access to a

constant supply of produce for the market. Indeed, it
may be seen as a mark of success of Lu's enterprise.
Again it appears as if his independence in this respect
could be correlated to his earlier entrepreneurial
background in his native district of Zhongshan.[3]

Needless to say, not only Keng Hau farmers come to
sell their produce in Sha Tin Market. The recruitment
of marketers is valley-wide. For instance, Ma Hua, who
lives high up on the slopes of To Fong Shan overlooking
the Pak Tin valley, tries, in the first place, to sell
his vegetables in Sha Tin Market, although he lives far
off; he, or his wife, has to walk a steep and incon-
venient path carrying the heavy baskets. If Ma goes
himself he may load the baskets on his bicycle for the
last stretch of road whereas his wife walks. (Rural
Chinese women never seem to use bicycles as a means of
transportation.) Even native villagers, like Wei
Chunshang of Tin Sam, aim at the local market if this
seems feasible.

Sha Tin Market seems to have a good reputation among
vegetable farmers as a place where it is relatively
easy to sell. It is not possible for us to verify such
pronouncements but the fact that it is reasonably easy
for the farmers to sell directly to the consumer
suggests that Sha Tin is, at least, as good a place as
any other market town in the New Territories, but
probably better than most.

The marketing organization, i.e. the Sha Tin Rural
Committee, extracts a small fee for all produce sold in
the market by way of a compulsory weighing operation.
The charge by the seller is five cents per catty, which
commission is for welfare programmes in the district.[4]
Vegetables sold to the stalls will certainly have to
pass through the official weighing, whereas it seems
more doubtful whether the hawkers always care about this
market regulation.

There is no marketing legislation to prevent the
farmer from retailing his own produce:

> Nothing in these regulations shall be construed to
> prevent or restrict within the New Territories Area
> or the Kowloon Area - (a) the sale retail of any
> vegetables by the producer thereof . . .[5]

Notwithstanding this the Keng Hau farmers claim that
their selling activities on the sea-front path are
illegal. At the same time all agree that control is
extremely lax, and that there is no interference from
the police, nor are bribes in any form necessary. If

something should turn up the strategy employed by the
hawkers will be that of *zou gui* - 'roaming spirits' -
that is, instant retreat. No one has been able or
willing to state what the illegal element is. What may
be referred to is the fact that the farmers do not have
hawkers' licences. But it seems very questionable
whether they actually need any sort of permit although
they think they do.

Business in Sha Tin is quite limited, naturally, and
it is not possible for the market here to avail itself
of the local produce. Then the alternative is the metropolitan market of Kowloon with its large and continuous
demand for fresh vegetables. But the city is distant
and the markets there not easily accessible for the Sha
Tin countrymen. The official avenue to these marketing
assets is the Vegetable Marketing Organization (VMO).
This is a governmental agency designed to deal with all
wholesale transactions of vegetables in Kowloon and the
New Territories; it has a sole franchise founded on the
law of Hong Kong. The legal framework provides for a
complete governmental control of the movement of
vegetables within the Colony, with the exception of Hong
Kong Island.

> No person shall, except under and in accordance with
> a permit in writing issued by or on behalf of the
> Director (of the VMO) sell vegetables wholesale in
> the Kowloon Area or in the New Territories Area,
> except at a wholesale vegetable market.[6]

The VMO marketing system is closely linked to a
number of marketing co-operative societies in the New
Territories. There are in all (in 1970) 31 such bodies,
and one of these operates in Sha Tin. This organization has an office located in Tung Lo Wan village.
The delivery takes place in the early morning. There
are a number of collection stations spread around the
valley and the farmers bring their baskets to these.
They load a VMO lorry which passes by these stations
on a scheduled and regular circuit. The vegetables are
brought to the office building where the contents are
weighed and farmers' receipts issued. Then the lorry
sets out for the VMO wholesale market operating in Sham
Shui Po.

Transportation is free in the sense that there is no
direct fee and the lorries are supplied by the Vegetable
Marketing Organization. Earlier this government agency
had its own fleet of vehicles but this scheme was
changed later and the organization now leases lorries

from commercial companies. We have been told that the
reason for this change of policy was that the collection stations tended to proliferate generally – often
according to the changes of leaders in the co-
operatives – and the steady increase in numbers of
stations along narrow dirt tracks made the big VMO
lorries difficult to handle. There was also an ever-
increasing demand for more lorries. The marketing
organization still pays the bill for transportation.
A farmer must not necessarily be a member of a co-
operative society to make use of the VMO facilities,
but official statistics show that 83 per cent of the
produce delivered to the government market comes from
co-operative members.

The vegetables are brought to the big market halls
in Sham Shui Po where retailers and hawkers come to
buy their daily supplies. Later in the afternoon the
same day the gains are paid to the farmer through the
co-operative office. The Vegetable Marketing Organization handles imported produce also, and this –
generally coming from China – is sold in competition
with the greens brought in from the New Territories.
The VMO levies a commission of 10 per cent of the
selling price for ordinary vegetables and of 20 per
cent on special kinds of high quality, like tomatoes.
This applies to domestic produce as well as imported.
In fact, the commission on imports subsidizes the
otherwise uneconomical marketing system; although it
is generally held among farmers that imported vegetables should not be handled by the VMO as they affect
the selling prices in a negative way, some important
benefits are at hand. The free transportation and the
economic support of the co-operatives are attractive
assets for the New Territories' farmers. But in Sha
Tin this is not so. Very few vegetable growers we know
of use the VMO facilities regularly, if at all.

If we turn to Keng Hau we find that no immigrant
farmer among the households we have investigated there
uses the Vegetable Marketing Organization and the
Co-operative Society at all. Two main reasons for
this are, according to the information provided by the
farmers, that "it takes too much trouble and time" and
"it gives a lower profit" as compared with other
marketing procedures. We believe there is some substance in these claims. It takes a long time for a
farmer to get his cash after he has delivered his
produce to the collection station of a Co-operative.
And, we may infer from a great number of conversations,

it seems as if the vegetable gardener feels that after
handing over his crop to the co-operative people and
receiving his receipt he has no real control over what
happens. In fact, if he has bad luck and his vegetables are of inferior quality he may discover that
they cannot be sold and are therefore dumped into the
sea. And why this happens is not so easy for the
producer to grasp, and suspicions of carelessness or
even dishonesty arise easily. Other factors may be
involved as well. It is understood that the drivers
and workers on the lorries, true urbanites from the
metropolis of Kowloon, do not have a very high opinion
of the rustic people providing their loads. As one
informant put it: "The farmers are treated like cows
and dogs." Perhaps this is an overstatement but
nevertheless we must acknowledge that fear of disrespect and incidents of bad treatment are important
factors affecting marketing planning.

It has been suggested that political opinions affect
also the Sha Tin marketing situation. Left-wing
sympathies are strong in the valley and this, so we are
told, may mean that farmers, on political moral principles, avoid dealing with government agencies. This
is, however, rather doubtful. Although it may be part
of individual motivation, there is nothing to suggest
that there is anything like an anti-VMO campaign, let
alone an organized boycott. The Co-operative is under
Communist management and VMO board members also show a
strong left-wing leaning.

There has been reason to stress already that
although the local Sha Tin market is of great importance, it cannot avail itself of the locally-grown
produce, and access to the metropolitan markets is
something that is vital for many farmers. If the
official, legal VMO way of achieving this end is dismissed there are other illegal alternatives to which
the vegetable grower turns.

One of these procedures is known as the *hei
shichang* - 'black market place.' This refers to illegal
wholesale marketing carried out by urban businessmen who
operate generally from the Sham Shui Po area. The
traffic is well organized. In the Keng Hau area there
are three competing private marketing enterprises. Each
has its own lorry for the transportation of vegetables
into Kowloon. The lorry crews place big bamboo baskets
alongside the access road to one of the villages, each
basket marked by the character for the owner's surname
painted in black. The farmers can bring their produce

to this place and select baskets according to the markings and their own preference of business partners. Special tags are distributed and the farmer jots down his name (or his mark) and ties it to those baskets he will make use of. Most farmers keep such labels in their cottages and many keep a stock of the businessmen's baskets in their backyards in order to make the marketing preparations easier.

All these activities take place during the night and the lorries leave Keng Hau in the early morning a few hours before dawn. A representative of the businessman returns in the afternoon to distribute the profit, which amounts to 95 per cent of the selling price of the produce delivered, the remaining five per cent being the commission of the illegal marketing organization.

This description provides a theme which occurs with slight variations all over the area. Sometimes it is claimed that the commission charged is ten per cent and watercress specialists in the Kak Tin-San Tin area who deal with one middleman operating in Tai Kok Tsui in Kowloon are charged 'for the transportation' of their produce, a fee of 50 cents per bundle of watercress containing perhaps 10 catties. This seems to be a relatively fixed price. The bundles cannot be tied too big as they must keep their shape under the handling in the market to fetch a good price.

It is not easy to trace the main operators of the illegal private marketing. A number of such middlemen are employees of the government's Vegetable Marketing Organization, running their own private business as a most important sideline. The main feature of their contacts with the producers is the maintenance of the farmers' trust. In Sha Tin where there is little competition from the official marketing through the Co-operative Society, they still have to reckon with competition between themselves as a factor of importance, and they must maintain a reputation of efficiency and honesty. The farmer, on the one hand, may see an advantage in sticking to one particular dealer as he may look upon the enterprise as a potential source of credit. The businessman, on the other hand, will ensure himself of a steady supply and therefore prefers to deal on a regular basis with producers he knows well. Often this marketing system is an open one characterized by slight competition between a limited number of businessmen. Sometimes, as is the case with those who handle the marketing of watercress from the specialized farms in the Kak Tin-San Tin area, the system is more closed and access to their services is available only through

introduction of earlier clients. As Liu Lang of that
area said: "The middleman is not a countryman from my
own district, but I have known him for a very long time,
and the first time I met this person was through the
recommendations of friends." 'Landmannschaft' -
xiangli - is mentioned sometimes as a notion generating
mutual trust and manifestations of trust between farmers
and businessmen, but the limited number of marketing
operators may tend to limit the importance of the norm
in this context.

Although the *hei shichang* procedure is reputed to be
reliable in that all vegetables delivered are being
sold, and efficient in that the farmer gets his money
the same day, it is, nevertheless, a second choice. To
bring the crops to the local markets is stressed nearly
always as a more expedient way of selling. It is only
when the local markets cannot swallow rich harvests that
the metropolitan markets must come into focus.
Undoubtedly the farmer's household saves time by the use
of a middleman, but this advantage may be negated by
another factor. In our conversations with a number of
people from all over the valley we found no negative
attitudes referring to the marketers. Deng Fen of Keng
Hau with his large land-holdings and correspondingly
large yields finds the selling through middlemen the
only efficient way of handling the marketing problem,
and in all respects the best solution.

Most people who use the *hei shichang* arrangements,
however, claim intermittently that they hesitate to use
these middlemen. The main argument against them was
given, among others, by Wu An: "I do not trust the
black market as I cannot know exactly what the prices
are, and I fear I will be cheated." It seems as if
Chen Quan's statement that "only when we are in
difficulties we will use them as we will get less from
them" applies generally to the farming households in
Keng Hau - with Deng Fen as a notable exception. But
if we turn to men like Lu Taiyun, who never use the
services of middlemen, they are emphatically negative.
"If I sell my produce through the black market, I will
be cheated about the price, and the dealers also
manipulate the weighing." But Lu can sneer confidently
at these people as he operates one market stall of his
own in each of the two towns and does not need to rely
on others.

Chen Quan in Keng Hau is one of those gardeners in
the valley who try to reach the more profitable urban
markets directly themselves without employing the
ready-made services of other people. Intermittently he

or his wife will take their harvests to the metropolitan
area of Hongkong where they hawk their supply themselves
in the streets, preferably in the regions of North Point
and Western District. They claim that an expedition of
this kind will give a return of about HK$40, which could
be compared with the approximately HK$15[7] to be gained
in the local Sha Tin Market in one day. It is obvious
then that although the costs for this direct marketing –
transportation, meals in food shops, bribes to hawker
police, loss of valuable time – add up a substantial
bill, it is still well worthwhile.

But the prerequisite is that the harvest is ample so
that they can sell at least 40 catties a day – otherwise,
it is claimed, it is not profitable. In order to bring
their produce to the city they employ a private lorry.
This is a van which brings fresh fish every morning from
Kowloon to Sha Tin, and instead of returning empty, the
driver provides transportation for some farmers, as a
private sideline. Chen Quan and his wife know this
driver well and if they wish to make use of the fish
lorry they bring their vegetables to Tai Wai around
eight o'clock in the morning and wait until he passes by.
Such a marketing expedition takes about ten hours.

As this procedure is illegal in two respects – it
entails unlicensed movement of vegetables out of the New
Territories to Hong Kong Island and also unlicensed
hawking in the streets – it is not without risks. We
have mentioned already bribery as one of the costs which
go with this kind of marketing. The police-like hawker
control units are readily bought off and the sums
involved are not said to be heavy – 'a few dollars'.
But sometimes luck is bad. Chen Quan's wife was once
arrested and had to appear in court the following day
where she was fined HK$10. She lost also the travelling
expenses for the journey to town and one day's labour,
apart from the loss and effort going with the marketing
expedition. The event is talked about with a great deal
of bitterness. And many are the stories told about
patrolmen who turn hawkers' baskets upside down and step
on their contents. Such measures of confiscation can be
observed intermittently in the street markets of Kowloon
and Hongkong.

Flowers are gathered in the evening and tied into
bundles which are brought to collection stations for
transportation to the wholesale market in Kowloon.
Transport is provided by lorries owned by individuals or
by bodies of people representing different interests.
In the Keng Hau area at least five lorries operate in

the flower business. There is one which belongs to a
'left-wing' association, a Communist *gonghui* or labour
union; another is operated by a 'right-wing', National-
ist-loyal union. Two are 'neutral' vans used in
private commerce. The fifth one - about which we know
very little, unfortunately, - is said "to belong to a
village." We have not been able to discern any prefer-
ences of the farmers to accord with the ownership of
the vehicles. For instance, Chen Quan, who is a firm
anti-communist, generally uses a 'left-wing' lorry from
Tai Wai. The departure from Sha Tin is about half an
hour past midnight and the fee charged is generally
HK$1.50 for produce and one accompanying person, and
HK$2 if two persons travel together.

The prosperous and technically-minded farmer, Ye
Wanzhe in Pak Tin, has his own transportation, a
Morris station-wagon. Few farmers can afford such an
expedience.

The main flower market is located on Boundary Street
in upper Kowloon during the night and hundreds of
farmers come together here to sell their flowers to
middlemen, retailers and hawkers. The market operates
every night and is managed by a Fresh Flower Association.
Most producers of Keng Hau are members of this society,
but membership is not a prerequisite as the market is
open to everyone who has flowers to sell. It is often·
claimed that no stable links exist between retailers
and brokers on the one hand, and producers on the other.
The buyers in the market tend to circulate and buy a
few bunches from each seller. This means that by and
large no one bringing flowers to the market will return
entirely empty-handed, unless the market demand is
extremely low. However, a very good informant from Tin
Sam, a native from the Wei lineage there, who has taken
up flower farming in recent years, reports that when
the growers have placed their produce on the pavement
of the street they are approached by their regular
dealers. He himself prefers that kind of informal
arrangement as it provides convenience and some
security - the dealer is more or less obliged to buy
from him even if the market is oversupplied and prices
are low. Thus we may, on such information as we have,
only conclude at this stage that marketing practices
vary.

Generally illegal marketing is limited to a short
period every year - the Chinese New Year season. At
this time the farmers bring their flowers into the
metropolitan areas where they hawk them at strategic
locations. A great deal of the flower gardening is

aimed at the New Year festive season. Planting is so
planned as to supply the farmer with an ample harvest
just in time for these lucrative days. Everyone in
Hong Kong who can afford to do so buys fresh flowers
or small potted trees to celebrate the arrival of a new
moon year. Flower markets are arranged in public open
places and spring up 'spontaneously' in the streets.
This is not only a Hong Kong feature; the flower markets
in Canton, for instance, have a long reputation as
crowded and noisy places of gaiety at this season. The
women in the Keng Hau neighbourhood maintain a constant
interest in the New Year business and continue a year-
round discussion as to what locations will turn out to
be the best places for hawking flowers next New Year.

So far we have presented a descriptive outline of the
marketing activities of the Sha Tin, and especially the
Keng Hau farmers. We believe that marketing processes,
from an anthropologist's viewpoint, may be understood
largely on a level of conscious motivation. The
sequence of events we perceive of in this context may be
seen as emerging from consecutive strategic choices
pertaining to procedures, middlemen, and consumers. In
this essay our main focus is on the rural producers. We
have found that a number of alternatives are at hand and
we have arrived at the general opinion that the
alternative chosen is always the one that gives the
opting person the highest profit. This does not necessarily mean that the calculation is 'objective' - there
is little to suggest that there exists in the mind of
each actor a complete knowledge of how all the different
alternatives would work out for him personally. Each
marketing option contains, in this respect, a certain
amount of chaos. But the 'entropy' pertaining to these
different situations varies with each marketer according
to his particular background experience and his acquired
knowledge.

In most cases we have found that the producers show a
strong preference for retailing their own produce
directly to the consumer. Such transactions take place
in the local market town which is well known to all
farmers, and there, in the tea houses and in the streets,
it is easy to learn the current market prices. Of
course, saleable prices are not directly fixed by an
'objective' law of supply and demand, but rather by ideas
and estimates relating to how much produce has been
brought to one particular market place and how many
people may be willing to pay for the available produce.
The farmer who brings vegetables to Sha Tin Market can
make fair predictions of his success and his gains from

what he can observe himself and from what he hears from
other hawkers, stall keepers, and in the tea houses.
And he can follow events in the market continuously,
even if he does not go there every day, from reports of
his neighbours and friends. Events in the local market
are predictable and the farmers can control the situation
to a large extent. [8]

We have seen in this chapter that when a vegetable
gardener transgresses the framework of the local marketing
facilities, this is due generally to his awareness that
his harvest is too big for a country town of limited business. If he wants to remain inside that local framework,
and thereby retain a great amount of control over
marketing events, his solution may be to intensify his
local marketing by way of selling to licensed dealers or
by setting up a permanent stall. But in situations when
the local market towns cannot avail themselves of the
local produce most farmers look to the metropolitan areas
across the range of mountains which separate the New
Territories from the city of Kowloon. But the events in
the metropolitan markets are highly unpredictable; the
vegetable market of Hong Kong is continuously rocked by
the uneven imports from China.

To our knowledge there are two main avenues providing
access to the city markets. One is endowed with official
monopoly and is a governmental sponsored wholesale
Vegetable Marketing Organization. Its big market hall is
filled with produce mainly from the many marketing
co-operative societies of the New Territories. The other
main channel is through illegally operating vegetable
dealers who provide transportation and the service of
selling. A main difference between the two lies in the
circumstances that the VMO does not take on any responsi-
bility for the vegetables delivered. They belong to the
farmers and the organization is there to provide
marketing facilities for producers and retailers alike.

When competition is hard owing to a great output of
New Territories greens and vast imports from China
(which passes through the same marketing organization),
and when freshness and quality are not up to the buyer's
standards, there is no guarantee whatsoever that the
farmer's harvest will be sold at all. As it is no use
bringing the vegetables back into the countryside to wait
for new opportunities in the following days, the unsold
remains, which may be sizeable, are destroyed. In
comparison with the highly unpredictable VMO market, the
private nightly operations by illegal businessmen offer
more security. They sell everything delivered although
bad quality produce may fetch very low prices.

Again, the illegal business offers other less attractive
aspects. If the VMO, at least theoretically, provides
the farmer with an insight into marketing procedures and
prices, the illegal traffic cuts him off from all information on current prices in that he must rely solely on
what the merchant says. The openly-stated commission
requested by the dealer is accepted as fair, but in
addition to that the farmer feels that there is much
dishonesty involved. By and large, the weighing of the
produce delivered is considered unfair and, again, there
is no possibility for the producer to check on prices
quoted. The farmer's control of the events pertaining
to the metropolitan marketing is limited in the extreme.

Why then do the Keng Hau farmers prefer the illegal
middlemen to the official marketing organization? In
their balance of pros and cons they find one striking
difference between the two in that the co-operative
society - the Sha Tin end of the VMO operations - is an
organisation whereas the vegetable dealer is a person.
It is true to say that the farmers tend to allocate
trust to individuals rather than to public corporations.
Misgivings and considerations apart, some degree of
trust is still needed and a personal relationship[9] is a
better medium for the transfer of such expectations than
are impersonal bonds which link the producer to an
office. We should note also that one important factor
which makes illegal private marketing highly competitive
is the relative closeness of the metropolitan area,
which circumstance lowers the transportation costs and
makes free lorry-freight less essential. In Fan Leng
and Tai Po, for instance, the co-operatives are much
stronger organizations.

The only way to make metropolitan marketing at
least approximately as predictable as the local Sha Tin
trading for the farmer is for him to bring the produce
himself to the city area and there hawk it in the
streets, selling directly to the consumers. The fact
that most people do not bother may be due to a general
lack of strategic knowledge of the cities - knowledge
of where to hawk, how to deal with hawker control, and
how to behave to customers and competitors.

The flower market does not present any alternative
ways of reaching customers. All business is done in
the city area by the producer-seller himself. Marketing
of flowers is equally predictable or unpredictable for
all who participate.

To understand the nature of vegetable marketing we
must recognize the key factor, which is that the farmers
sell a highly perishable product. There are no storage

facilities and no possibilities at all of holding back
a crop and wait for the right time to sell. As soon
as the vegetables are ripe for harvest, time is precious
and immediate marketing essential.[10] This fact
strengthens the position of brokerage, whether private
or co-operative in nature.

1. Barrow 1951:2.
2. Barrow 1952:7.
3. Aijmer 1973:66f.
4. Cf. Groves 1965a:19, and 1965b:22, for a similar arrangement in Tai Po.
5. *Agricultural Products (Vegetable Marketing) Regulations*, A3.
6. *ibid*. A3.
7. Cf. the discussion on incomes of Chapter II.
8. This does not mean that the hazard of the price fluctuations due to imports from China does not have an effect on the local market. More generally on market prices, see for instance Tax 1953:14ff and Firth 1966:225ff.
9. Still it must be emphasized that there is in present-day Sha Tin no code of social relations to interfere with and stabilize market prices as is often the case in communities which attach great importance to traditional forms of social intercourse in tight kin-ship dominated networks.
10. Fei & Chang (1947:191) discuss another aspect of time shortage in a marketing context. Sellers of home-made paper in Yunnan cannot stay in the market long enough to wait for individual buyers because the market is too far away from the home village. Thus they usually sell at wholesale. This way the paper brings a lower price and the vendors do not risk to have to take the whole load back. See also Gallin 1966:63 for other solutions to the problem of time.

VIII. THE DEVELOPMENT OF HORTICULTURE IN SHA TIN

A basic idea of traditional Chinese rural society in the Guangdong Province is that land is an agnatic source. Rice cultivation in flooded fields is everywhere endowed with special meaning. All activities related to the cultivation of rice draw meaning from their connection with the agnatic source. And as agricultural activities were a prominent feature of Guangdong village life we may say that traditional life was focused on an awareness of agnation. Kinship, in the present expressed in corporate lineage organizations, was linked to land and agriculture in many ways. The individual management of the fields by a gardener is not meaningful in the same way for the corporation of agnatic relatives, and it is not endowed with prestige, nor can it derive any meaning from lineage and agnatic ideology.

The ritualization of the lineage ideology and the ritualization of the rice cultivation are inseparable in that both are focused on dead forefathers.[1] Giving up rice production will for traditionalist villagers mean a break-up from a social situation dominated by traditional lineage aspirations and goals. The cultivation of rice has formed, to a very great extent, the essence and rhythm of life in the villages. The intimate connexion between the calendar, the cycle of festivals, and the process of rice cultivation gives a meaning to the rhythm of life which reaches far beyond what can be measured in terms of production and other economic categories. The transplantation of the first crop cannot be done before the *Qingming* festival; *Duanwu* precedes the first rice harvest and the sowing of the second crop. *Chongyang* precedes the second harvest. These important festivals are entirely isolated from the context of vegetable gardening which does not in the same way provide a fixed, seasonally repetitive pattern of activities. Through the use of many different species of vegetables, which can, in accordance with their ecological requirements, be introduced into a year-round production, the market gardener lives in a uniform and constant progression of acts concerned with his land. There is no peak season and no off season. There is nothing particular to look forward to, nor anything to talk about in retrospect on dry and cool winter days with fallow fields.

Contrariwise, the cultivation of rice provides a framework endowing meaning to social events and distributing them in time. Rice cultivation in this area combines two cyclic technical systems, nearly identical in nature, into one cultural and social system. Vegetable and flower growing combine many minor self-contained systems into an agglomeration which assumes no specific cultural or social form as an overall system. Each crop on each plot forms a province of meaning. These are discrete and not necessarily linked to each other. An integration is obtained only by way of converting these crops into cash. Even here the effective integration of the different provinces varies with the individual farmer.

At this point we must consider the decline of rice cultivation in the New Territories. When the British arrived at the turn of the century, rice was everywhere the predominant crop. Hillside fields were planted with vegetables mainly for the farmer's own consumption and for local village markets. At this time in Sha Tin, the balance between paddy fields and dry cultivation comes out strongly in favour of the former. A ten per cent sample of the registered landlots in three Demarcation Districts (182, 187, and 189) of the valley reveals that in 1905 a portion amounting to 91.7 per cent of the fields was under rice cultivation. The ratio expressed in terms of acres was 90.1 per cent to 9.9 per cent in favour of rice.

We have pointed out already that the growth of urban areas on the Kowloon Peninsula brought about a major change in the villages there, in that the farming community increasingly switched over to cash crops - vegetables to be marketed in the new and expanding urban areas. We do not know how this change came about, only that it happened in the near proximity of the urban markets. When the Kowloon-Canton railway was built through the New Territories there were some expectations that the vegetable farming zone would expand into that area as a new means of transportation was now at hand. J.D. Lloyd, the 1921 Census Commissioner, writes in a report:

> The opening of the Railway seems, contrary to expectations, to have produced very little change; market supplies for Hong Kong still come from the Canton Delta as before, and paddy still remains the predominant crop.[2]

It was not until the 1950s that vegetable and flower cultivation rapidly spread into the Sha Tin area to encroach on old rice land. Charles Grant supplied us with some land use maps from this period, which show that rice was still an important crop then.[3] But change was well under way. There are two parallel processes on the macro level, which we must understand as background for further inquiries into the mechanism for the drastic change in the agricultural landscape.

Let us first consider two facts - rice cultivation in the area was never very profitable, and landholdings were small in relation to a growing population. The increase in population between 1911 and 1931 was about 14 per cent. There was little space for an accompanying expansion of the arable land. The soil was not very suitable for wet rice and the yields were as low as 100-200 catties per *douzhong,* which compares unfavourably with the western plains of the New Territories, which produce 300-400 catties per *dou.*[4] The hillsides were increasingly exploited in that people of nearby villages collected firewood and grass for fuel to be sold in the new urban markets. However, the increase in population was experienced as a pressure on the economy in many villages.

Many took advantage of the new occupational choices offered in the city areas and they became urban workers, sailors, or emigres in overseas countries. We have not been in the position to trace the migratory movements from the Sha Tin villagers in the period before the Japanese Occupation.[5] The population figures given by the 1911 Census Report do not suggest any large-scale emigration, but more or less temporary absentees might well have been included as household members in the count. In 1921 and 1931 no sex ratio is given so these census reports provide no information in this respect. In the post-war years, however, emigration increased as the possibility of going to the United Kingdom for holders of British passports had a feverish effect on the New Territories villages.

It is well known that Chinese-style restaurants have mushroomed in Britain since the 1950s. By and large, people in the catering business are former rice peasants who have switched over to culinary activities, sophisticated enough to stand up to the palatal satisfaction of an inexperienced Western public. Rising costs of living, lack of arable land, and population growth are factors which together created a situation characterized by feminization of the farm work process,

and an increasing abandonment of land. In some
instances villagers in Tai Wai have sold off their
inherited land holdings to urban speculators and
deposited the money thus gained in a bank. They claim
that the interest gained this way surpasses the value
of the yield of rice on their former holdings.
Accompanying this decline in traditional farming is
the increasing financing of households by remittances
from Britain.

The other macro process of importance is the chain
of political events in the People's Republic of China.
I have discussed these briefly elsewhere.[6] Suffice it
here to stress the momentuous aspect of this process
that is a strong immigration into the Crown Colony of
Hong Kong.

It was in the situation outlined above that the
immigrants from China appeared on the scene asking for
tenancy rights. By letting land to tenants the owner
makes more money from his holdings than he can by
maintaining the traditional rice farming. This simple
fact underlies the predominant pattern of land tenure
in Sha Tin; native villagers let land to outsiders at
rents that equal or surpass the gains from two crops of
rice on that land. At the same time their own energy
is directed to other tasks, varying from overseas work
and cottage industry to long tea-house conversations or
gambling. Thus the native villager's answer to the
explosive city development was, in the first place, not
an adjustment in his agricultural production to meet
the emerging urban demands; instead, he converted the
traditional two rice crops into two 'crops' of cash,
and reoriented his own efforts towards urban or suburban occupations which provide new external incomes.

Although there was early official encouragement of
local production of vegetables in Hong Kong, for
instance by the setting up of the Vegetable Marketing
Organization (VMO) in 1946, there was very little
response among the village farmers.[7] For example, in
the village of Sha Tin Wai only six of the resident 67
'farming families' - of which 22 are outsider households, however - are engaged in agriculture, and only
three of these 'families' raise cash crops.[8] The
table below[9] shows the result of the social survey of
five villages to which we have referred previously.

The change in land use was brought about by the
immigrant tenants. As has been observed elsewhere[10]
a great many of the newcomers to Sha Tin are people of
a definite urban background. Those who are not urbanites
are generally influenced by or under the leadership of

men of urban experience. One could arrange the people
of the Keng Hau neighbourhood according to a continuum
model, where at one extreme one would have 'deep
involvement in urban business life', and at the other
extreme 'deep involvement in rural subsistence life'.
This accomplished, we would find that the persons who
are placed close to the first extreme function in
social networks which link them to the persons approach-
ing the extreme of rural ignorance. The flow of actions
in these networks reveals the former as informal leaders
and mentors for the latter. The sophisticated urbanites
are models for economic action and thus transmitters of
knowledge, both actively as formal advisers, and
passively as their gardens are observable phenomena from
the study of which one may learn a great deal. The
vegetable market garden is thus the businessman's enterprise disguised as a rustic farmstead. The emergence of
vegetable cultivation is an 'overspill' from the urban
areas. What we deal with is the city's adjustment to
the countryside rather than an adaptation of the rural
husbandry to meet urban demands.

Village	Total no. of Families	No. Engaged in Farming	Cash	Subsistence
Fui Yiu Ha	18	6	1	5
Sha Tin Wai	67	12	6	6
To Shek	21	20	-	20
Chap Wai Kan	9	6	1	5
Ngau Pei Sha	21	12	3	9

It is not true to say that rice peasants have not
switched over to vegetable cultivation at all. Obviously
this kind of person is not common in Sha Tin, but he
occurs and there are a few native vegetable growers in
nearly every village. Still it is a noteworthy fact that
the present village gardeners did not give up their rice
cultivation until they had precedent models for action in
the form of immigrant garden enterprises. Wei Chunshang
of Tin Sam, for instance, recalls that he found it quite
difficult to learn the skill of vegetable and flower
growing as his only previous experience was rice cultivation. But he maintains that the officers of the
Department of Agriculture had been quite helpful and
they supplied him with the fundamental knowledge of how
to grow the different kinds of greens. But he also
stresses that much of his present skill is derived from
the immigrants. The contacts between immigrants and

native villagers are extremely limited, and we must
therefore assume that the models were observed and that
what could not be observed had to be acquired from
other sources of knowledge, like the Department of
Agriculture. But surely the example of the immigrant
market garden was something to be envied and reproduced,
and thus a primary incentive for a new agricultural
order.

The villagers, both the majority who act as landlords
and the few who have followed the outsiders in taking up
gardening, remain within a system of meaning, linked
with the cultivation of rice. When today this underlying system is represented in social reality, forms
which are different from traditional representations are
generated. But the application of new external variables to the transformational process has not affected
the basic messages transformed, although they are acted
out differently. Thus land rent is collected on two
occasions, corresponding to the former two rice crops.
Furthermore, the emigrants return to the home village at
New Year, *Qingming*, the Dragon Boat Festival, and
Chongyang, even from faraway Britain. We have argued
elsewhere[11] that buildings form counterparts to land in
representing territorial belonging, mediated by way of
kinship; the emigrants' rebuilding of their inherited
houses thus reveals their continued social interest in
that belonging.

The immigrant gardener's outlook on life derives
meaning from the variety of events rather than from a
cyclic organization of occurrences. His garden enterprise is an agglomerate of small projects. Each crop
has its own investments, its own risks, and its own
gains or losses. If the farmer earlier has had a long
and deep engagement in business, he will be more apt to
integrate the many small systems of events that are the
crops into one system of management. To the extent
that the total farm business has not been integrated,
the gardener feels that economic life is a gambling
activity, and to him fate is of paramount importance.
The well-integrated farm enterprise contains, as it
were, little 'information', and the predictability of
the economic outcome makes a prosperous farmer. On
the other hand, the loose agglomerate type of farm
contains much 'information'. The outcome is unpredictable and the farmer generally poor and apathetic.

The only remedy for an existing lacuna of knowledge
is crop specialization as we have found it among the
watercress farmers, for instance. Specialization
reduces the demand for technical skill and increases

4. *The farm of Cheng Zhiming in the Keng Hau Neighbourhood. In the foreground is one of the very few remaining rice fields, behind which are fields of watercress*

the predictability of the economic future. On the other hand, it implies much less adaptability to the world; sudden bad market conditions may be disastrous, and any similar unexpected event will rock the whole enterprise and perhaps ruin the farmer.

What has been said here should be understood as generally applicable to flower cultivation also.

NOTES TO CHAPTER VIII

1. Cf. Aijmer 1964, 1968, 1976b, and n.d.
2. Lloyd 1921b: Intr. It has been estimated that prior to the Pacific War only some 20 per cent of the Hong Kong consumption of vegetables was locally grown.
3. Grant 1960: facing p.102.
4. Lai 1964:82.
5. Cf. my description of three Hakka mountain villages for an account of a similar but more intense process; Aijmer 1967. See also Watson 1975.
6. Aijmer 1973.
7. The aim may have been to bring about self-sufficiency in vegetables in the Colony. However, at times the official thinking seems to have been ambiguous. Thus it was stated at a Rotary Lunch by a high-ranking official that in times of emergency only rice could be the answer to the Colony's needs; *South China Morning Post,* February 11th, 1965.
8. Giles & Yung 1966, I:11.
9. Giles & Yung 1966, I:11; but note that the figures for Sha Tin Wai here are somewhat different. Note also that outsider families are counted in total numbers. Again, in the village of Kak Tin it was estimated that seven land owners out of ten had given up all farming completely. How correct this estimate is it is difficult to say.
10. Aijmer 1973:67
11. Aijmer 1975.

IX. SHA TIN IN A CHINESE CONTEXT

So far the aim of this essay has been to describe the
core of activities which characterize the vegetable and
flower gardening life in Sha Tin. In doing so we have
arrived at a number of conclusions which may merit some
further consideration.

We have observed that vegetable cultivation was not
very important traditionally in this area. The little
production that existed was mainly for local consumption.
We may assume that the possible market circulation of
vegetables was confined to local village markets like
those of Tai Wai and Tin Sam, which served local village
buyers. For purposes of comparison we may note that
Daniel H. Kulp describes a village market in northern
Guangdong where food-shops were selling vegetables and
other products:

> This provides village families with a wider range of
> selection of foods for their diets than would be
> possible were they compelled by the inconvenience of
> markets to depend solely on their own products. They
> grow a limited number of vegetables; other gardeners
> grow other kinds, and a monotonous diet is thus
> broken up by buying the different kinds of vegetables
> put on the market from other gardens.[1]

The vegetable cultivation that took place was thus
essentially inside the subsistence sphere.

Today market gardening and large-scale flower plantations dominate the rural landscape. This feature is
characteristic of the New Territories generally, with
the exception of the mountain areas and many of the out-
lying islands.

The general shift to market gardens and flower plantations should be understood against the background of
the proximity of the cities of Kowloon and Hongkong.
Vicinity to main urban centres is a traditional prerequisite for commercialized horticulture. Large cities
in China seem to have been surrounded by zones of
vegetable cultivation. This was so in Canton, for
instance:

> The city of Canton was ringed by a belt about five or
> six miles wide where vegetable gardens densely dotted
> the rustic scene . . . An enveloping belt of

vegetable farms around an urban center is an
ecological pattern characteristic of Canton as
well as other cities.[2]

But the belts of urban market influence were certainly
still wider. Thus the village of Nanching in Panyu
District just outside Canton was specializing in the
cultivation of leek, which was not only exported to the
nearby city but to Hong Kong and Macau as well.[3] Still,
the vegetable gardens had not eliminated the traditional
rice cultivation in this village.

On Honan Island, across the Pearl River from the city
of Canton, vegetable cultivation for the city markets
was an important feature also, but occupied only 30.2 per
cent of the arable land; 36.4 per cent was occupied by
rice.[4] We know that elsewhere in Guangdong there were
similar zones of market gardening around townships like
Shiqi and Shantou.[5] 'Phoenix Village' in northern
Guangdong specialized in market crops like fruits and
bamboo, but also vegetables. It was clearly inside a
cash crop zone centred on the Chaozhou and Shantou
markets.[6] From another area of China, Shandong, we
find evidence that the emergence of Qingdao as a modern
city affected the villagers of Taitou in a similar,
although less consistent way:

> Every year large quantities of farm products are
> sold to Tsingtao either directly by the farmers
> themselves or through the grain dealers and vegetable
> merchants. The farmer's inclination for growing
> special crops and raising certain livestock for the
> market in Tsingtao is becoming more obvious day by
> day. The increased acreage for growing soybeans,
> wheat, certain vegetables and fruits, and the
> increased amount of poultry and hogs is all due to
> the new market.[7]

Pater Stenz observed that market gardening occurred
in the nearness of big towns in the same province.[8] The
pattern is repeated again in the southwestern province
of Yunnan. On the basis of their field-work there, Fei
Hsiao-tung and Chang Chih-i generalize:

> The village is near a large walled town in which on
> every other day a market is held. Or the villagers
> may go to other markets nearby, as a round trip to
> these more distant markets takes only half a day.
> With markets near at hand, they can select those
> crops to grow which bring the highest returns. They

can grow less rice and other staple food crops for
themselves because they are able to count upon
buying them when needed in the market. Market
gardening develops in response to these conditions.[9]

Flower growing is perhaps even more tied to urban
centres. The New Year flower markets of Canton are
famous, and so are the specialized flower gardens at
Huadi and Pantang in suburban Canton.[10] The affluence
and sophistication of urban dwellers are the pre-
requisites for any market demand for fresh-cut flowers
and potted dwarfed trees. Flower hawkers appeared in
the streets of the newly-founded city of Victoria on
Hong Kong Island in the latter half of the last century,
a fact which suggests nearby gardens.[11]

Our reading of the descriptions of southeastern
China presented by Kulp and Yang suggests that market
gardening in the localities under their observation was
done by indigenous villagers, who were members of
lineage constellations of people rooted in their
ancestral land. But we do not know how and when the
market gardens came about or who opted initially for a
switch from rice to vegetables, or fruit, if there ever
was such a change. All we can say is that these
villages had intense contacts with an urban milieu.
From the Colony of Hong Kong we have evidence that
vegetable cultivation of importance existed in the
villages on Hong Kong Island and on Kowloon Peninsula
in the nineteenth century. Thus it is said about the
Ceung Sha Wan area:

> Even at the turn of the century . . . there was
> probably a greater production of vegetables than
> was usual for a rural area . . . Already some
> families, mainly it seems, the later arrivals,
> grew only vegetables and sold them in Sham Shui
> Po, and also in the central and western districts
> of urban Hong Kong Island.[12]

It is interesting to note that the vegetable specialists
were 'later arrivals'. We can combine this piece of
information with the further statement that the later
arrivals could not always get land of their own but had
to rent land from the 'clans' which were made up of
early settlers.[13]

It seems as if the newcomers were also in 'clan'
groupings which may suggest that they were lineage seg-
ments that had broken away from some distant rural
settlements. Alternatively it suggests that agnatic

kinship ties were factors of importance in the recruitment of outsiders to Cheung Sha Wan.[14] It is thus
possible that the more enterprising inhabitants of this
village who took the lead, which in due time resulted
in a general change to vegetable marketing for profit,
were to be found among these tenants and late arrivals.
We may hypothesize that conditions for the rise of
market gardening are advantageous in situations characterized by proximity to dense urban areas in combination
with immigrants as tenant farmers.[15]

We have pointed out that the emerging city of Kowloon
did not bring about an extension of the vegetable zone
beyond the mountains into the Sha Tin valley and into
the New Territories at large. Between the years 1906
and 1915 the British sector of the Kowloon-Canton Railway was constructed and this new means of transportation is supposed to have been a precondition for
economic growth in the area. Again, a main road
connecting Kowloon and Tai Po was laid out through Sha
Tin at the turn of the century. Jack M. Potter, in
search of such factors as have influenced the economic
development in the Yuen Long area of the western
stretch of the New Territories, suggests:

> The railroad ran through Tai Po and Sha Tin in the
> eastern part of the New Territories, and it is
> probably in this area, and not in the Yuen Long
> area, that the increased contact with the city first
> began to affect the peasant economy.[16]

If we relate this assumption to the same author's
suggestion that

> since the establishment of Kowloon as a major urban
> area in 1861, the vegetable gardening belt has
> gradually extended in a concentric circle into the
> New Territories,[17]

we are made to believe that Sha Tin is an area that was
included in the horticulture zone at an early stage.[18]
It is true that the British administration hoped for
such a development as is revealed by the comment by
J.D. Lloyd, quoted above (p.90). But all facts point
to a state of affairs characterized by little change in
land use. Rice cultivation remained the principal
crop in Sha Tin, and the only significant vegetable and
flower farming there before the Pacific War was that of
Ho Baixiung, mentioned in our earlier discussion. All

villagers of the area with whom we have spoken agree on
the absence of vegetable market gardening in those days.

This was hardly due to lack of transportation. In
fact, both people from the valley and the surrounding
mountains walked to the Kowloon markets in order to sell
firewood - so those markets were within reach even
before the new means of transport were available. We
must look for other factors, like social values, knowledge, and occupational alternatives to farming, to
understand why economic development in terms of agricultural change did not come about in Sha Tin. Even in
the late 1950s large areas remained under rice cultivation.

We have found that there is a general rotation of
crops, but one with many variations. During the first
half of the year the fields are dominated by beans and
gourds on bamboo trellises, while the latter half of
the year is primarily the season of flowers. Flower
cultivation is a special feature of Sha Tin, although
it may be found on a small scale in many places of the
New Territories. Obviously it largely replaces the
cultivation of green-leafed vegetables commonly grown
in the cool season. If we compare the Sha Tin cycle
with that of the village of Nanching in Panyu we find
some similarity, derived from similar ecological
conditions.[19]

Drawing on a rather different field experience,
Morton H. Fried has suggested that:

> Operating his farm on the basis of cash crops, the
> farmer places the greatest portion of his land into
> the production of one or two staple items, the market
> value of which is high. The system is quite general
> in contemporary Chinese culture.[20]

In his own field in Anhui Province, however, cash crops
were minor: tobacco, choice bamboo, fruit, and
chrysanthemum for tea flavouring. But in that area rice
may be regarded as a cash crop, as more than fifty per
cent of crops in good years were exported.[21] In Sha Tin
the gardeners exhibit a more complex pattern of land use
which goes much beyond a simple concentration on one or
two staple items, a phenomenon described by Fried as
quite general. Fried's reasoning applies only if we
think of the items in terms of categories rather than in
terms of specific kinds. In this sense we will find
'bamboo trellis vegetables' as a major item and flowers
as the other. These two main categories tend to split
the farmer's year into two seasons reckoned according

to the crop rotation cycle. Simultaneously, seasons
are perceived in terms of climatic conditions and input
of work.

Knowledge and skill limit the market gardener's
choice of vegetables and flowers to be planted on his
land. The immigrant's background is important with
respect to what gardening skills prevailed in his
native district. The knowledge he acquired in the
place where he was born and raised is a repository which
can be drawn on in his new setting. Some authors writing
on Chinese rural conditions are prone to stress this
background knowledge. Potter, for instance, writes,

> These refugees came from villages near urban areas
> in China (particularly Canton) where there was a
> long tradition of vegetable growing for city markets,
> and they were well versed in the skills and techniques
> of the truck-gardening business.[22]

It is not to be doubted that inside the vegetable belt
centred on Canton there existed a widespread and varied
knowledge of horticulture. In Nanching in Panyu District,
practically every peasant family used part of the farm
for vegetable gardening.[23] There were five main types
of vegetables, each represented by several kinds.

But in Sha Tin many market gardeners are recruited
from regions which are well outside the vegetable zones
of Canton and other big cities. It seems as if vegetable cultivation in other areas was less common, and
rice was the predominant crop in the native districts
of most of our informants. Subsidiary crops existed
though, often of a regional character, like watercress
in Dongguan. Primary knowledge does not account alone
for the cultivation skill of the market gardeners in
Hong Kong. We have not much experience of the Yuen Long
plain, but obviously Potter's reasoning cannot fully
explain the presence of horticultural ability among the
New Territories immigrants.

We have argued that much of the immigrant's knowledge
is acquired in his new place of residence. On the one
hand such knowledge is arrived at by observation of
models in the form of earlier established market
gardeners. On the other hand, knowledge is tapped from
the immigrant's network of social relations. This network may include officers of the Government's Department of Agriculture. Of course, experimentation should
not be dismissed from consideration, but we find it
hard to believe that experimentation takes place in
isolation from knowledge transmitted over social net-

works. Thus not only background knowledge, but also
the extension of the immigrant's social contacts de-
limit the choices of vegetables and flower species and
these two factors account for the differentiated
appearance of the farms.

Our study suggests that a household of two adults
and some children will need at least four *douzhong* of
land for gardening.[24] When horticulture is a subsidiary occupation for only some of the household
members, while others are town employees, the size is
about two *dou*. A single person seems able to handle
two or three *dou* of land with only limited help.
Marjorie Topley, in her economic survey of the New
Territories, arrives at similar conclusions.

> An average size holding for an unattached male is
> about two *táu-chúng,* and for a family of four or
> five about four *táu-chúng*. With two *táu-chúng* an
> unattached man would be fairly fully employed . . .
> and could earn enough to support himself. The same
> applies to a family of four or five with four *táu-
> chúng* . . . The optimum size of vegetable fields
> with present methods of cultivation tends to be
> determined primarily by the number of persons avail-
> able to work the land.[25]

In the village of Yuts'un in the province of Yunnan
the size of the vegetable gardens was very similar to
what is found in the New Territories:

> A household of five has, on the average, three adult
> gardeners. Each adult can care for two *mow* of
> garden. The limit is therefore 6 *mow* of garden land,
> one-tenth of that of the rice farms. In actual fact,
> the largest truck garden in Yuts'un is only 4.8 *mow*.[26]

Land rents vary a great deal according to the natural
conditions and the whim of the land owner. Some of the
latter do not care about rent at all while others regard
their fields as a good source of profit. The rent is
generally paid in two installments which correspond to
the former rice crops on the land. Sometimes the rent
is still paid in the form of unhusked rice, a fact which
further stresses the continuous presence of a rice
tradition among the villagers. Potter has noted similar
circumstances in Ping Shan in the early 1960s.[27] He
found that the amount of rent continues to be based on,
and calculated in accordance with, the old agricultural
system of two rice crops a year. Rent can be paid in

grain or in cash according to what crops are grown.
This mode of thinking has kept land rents low; they
have not risen to parallel the increase in crop value
which follows from the introduction of vegetables.
This, however, applies only to indigenous village
tenants. Otherwise the price policy is different.

> If land is rented to new tenants (especially out-
> siders) for vegetable growing, the traditional rent
> is often considerably increased. The new tenants
> usually pay their rent in cash and, at present
> (1961-63), the rent charged by village landlords on
> vegetable fields rented to outsiders varies from a
> minimum of $100 to a maximum of $400 per d.c. *(douzhong)*
> per year, depending upon the quality of the field.[28]

We have seen that in Sha Tin also the increased rents
for outsider tenants are sometimes calculated in terms
of grain. The rents often surpass what the landowner
could gain from having the same land under rice cultivation with the yield of two annual crops. Roughly we
may estimate the vegetable farmer's rent to some twenty
per cent of the crop value. Thus land rent has not
followed the rise in value of the land. Chen Han-seng
points to a transitional system of payment in Guangdong
Province before the Pacific War. There was a tendency
to substitute payment in grain for payment in cash, but
the amount of rent was settled in terms of grain,
estimated at the price prevailing at the time of the
highest quotation, in the spring.[29] As far as I know,
a similar 'transitional stage' has not been introduced
in Sha Tin nor in the New Territories at large. The
tenant pays in grain or a fixed cash rent. The swiftness
of change in land use in Hong Kong has brought out
rapidly and clearly that land values are not related only
to potential crops.
We have found that tenancy rights to land give simultaneous rights to the irrigation system serving that
land. Unless a person does not farm a considerable
stretch of land he is not apt to invest in well-digging.
The acquisition of diesel pumps for irrigation purposes
was confined in time to the period when the gardeners
were competing with indigenous rice peasants. A handful
of vegetable and flower cultivators with no direct
access to water have introduced irrigation by way of
sprinkler systems. This has been achieved by way of
co-operation with and financial support from the Department of Agriculture. Jack Potter has traced the
introduction of pumps in Ping Shan, where the first one

was bought by a native villager who is one of the most successful farmers and the acknowledged informal leader of the village farmers. This man was followed by his two brothers and one other man, totalling four pumps. Potter's interpretation is that

> the innovation was probably adopted, not merely for utilitarian reasons, but because the new pumps were prestige symbols.[30]

Whatever prestige is implied in the ownership of a diesel pump, in Sha Tin it is the outsiders who enjoy this mark of distinction. Seemingly, different causes in the two areas have produced pump irrigation.

To start a vegetable and flower garden requires the possession of capital. The capital invested in tools can vary considerably. Other investments are fertilizers and insecticides. Owing to the farmer's informal handling of economic data it is difficult to estimate costs in market gardening generally. In 1959, official estimates were that an immigrant family of six needed about HK$2,130 to start planting four *douzhong* with vegetables. This figure includes the construction of a cottage.[31] Today it is definitely much more costly to get established.

We have noted already that Jack Potter encountered difficulties similar to ours in obtaining precise information in his field-work in Ping Shan, where most farmers flatly refused to give any estimates at all saying that there were simply too many variables involved. In spite of this, Potter goes on to construct an ordered picture of the economics of horticulture, and of course, this is very useful. He does not, however, pursue his important finding relating to the unsystematic nature of the knowledge of market-garden economics in the minds of market gardeners to find out what bearings this phenomenon has on our understanding of economic life in the New Territories.

C.K. Yang points out that in Panyu District outside Canton, vegetable cash crops required heavy investment in fertilizer, labour, and additional equipment. Because the average peasant was short of capital, his ability to raise vegetables was restricted.[32] Whether a person in Hong Kong is a rice peasant or an urban worker he will similarly need capital for initial investments in vegetable farming. In Sha Tin this prerequisite has not had the same sort of restricting effect as in Panyu. The lack of capital may stop indigenous villagers from entering the gardening business, but it has not restrained

urbanites with savings or credit from moving into the
countryside which has seen nearly a complete transition
in land use.

Incomes are also handled informally. A reasonable
estimate of a minimal yield is HK$1,000 per *douzhong* a
year. However, we think that the net profit is often
considerably higher. Potter has estimated a net gain
of HK$2,251 from the vegetable cultivation on one *dou*
for a year.[33] We guess that the profit margins were
narrower in 1969 than when Potter obtained his information in 1961. Potter's estimates largely confirm our
own guesswork.

The Sha Tin farmer can obtain credit from the market
town shops, but only at a cost in that prices for
things he will be obliged to buy from them will be
slightly higher for him than for the ordinary customer.
Discussing shops providing commodities on credit,
Marjorie Topley suggests that

> credit may require a guarantor or *taam-pó-yan*. He
> will be a person known to both creditor and debtor,
> and it is usual for the debtor to give him a gift
> for his services. The *taam-pó* system enables a
> small creditor to have a circle of debtors much
> wider than if operations were restricted only to
> those known to him personally.[34]

Our inquiries in Sha Tin about go-betweens acting on
behalf of the shops gave a negative result. It was
maintained that "the merchants know all the farmers in
Sha Tin, and therefore there is no need for middlemen."
The farmer acquires the status of a client qualified
for credit by way of being a regular customer for some
time. This difference from Topley's account may be due
to the fact that the Sha Tin Market is a recent phenomenon, although some of the shops are older than the
present market town. It is a small place with a limited
hinterland. The middleman strategy may have been
employed in the early fifties when the merchants were
more eager to extend credit. If so, it has nowadays
become an obsolete practice. However, it should be
pointed out that Topley's account is not based on a
study of any particular set of shops.

Barbara E. Ward describes a shop in a fishing
village, Kau Sai, in the Rocky Harbour region of the
New Territories. This shop is situated on the shore of
the anchorage and it provides its customers with lesser
fishing equipment. Much of its trade is done on credit.
The shop keeper exacts no interest on credit sales, nor

does he charge a higher price for what he sells. The
debts are probably hardly ever completely settled.
People pay what they can and when they can. The shop
keeper, who knows all his debtors personally, does not
force them to pay.[35] Here the shop keeper is inside a
tight network of social relations, entailing kinship
and close friendship. This circumstance accounts for
his inability to make credit increase his profit.
Potter points to similar mechanisms in Ping Shan.[36]

In Sha Tin merchants are generally Chaozhou men and
outsiders. They seek profit but are also anxious about
the continuity of business. The content of their networks of relations does not bar them from the exercise
of business principles. On the contrary, the basis for
their networks is their economic activities. That shop
keepers give money loans to needy farmers is a traditional feature well documented in the literature.[37]
Here it may be of interest to draw attention to the
fact that, as far as our knowledge goes, the Sha Tin
shops are not operating as banks. Potter hints at the
banking practices of the stores in the market town of
Yuen Long:

> in traditional times they deposited funds in some of
> the market town stores for safety and gradually drew
> on this account to make purchases in the store.[38]

We are not informed how these deposits were used by the
merchants.

From another part of China, Shandong, we learn that

> since most of the store proprietors in the market
> town have families in the surrounding villages, they
> are usually related to the farmers or know them well.
> It is customary for farmers who have surplus money to
> deposit it in the store run by a kinsman or fellow
> villager; the store, in turn, lends the money to its
> good customers, thus taking the place of a pawnshop.[39]

Again we must stress that the shop keepers of Sha Tin
are outsiders with no kinship ties to the villages of
the valley. Most shops are fairly new and social
relations maintained over longer spans of time are
comparatively rare. The relatively short distance to
Kowloon certainly means that Sha Tin people buy many commodities in the city and therefore are not interested in
deposits in particular shops in Sha Tin. Those immigrant
farmers who have any savings at all hide their cash at
home in the cottage. They do not use the branch office

of the Hong Kong and Shanghai Bank since the closure in 1965 of the Canton Trust Bank, the only official banking institution in Sha Tin. However, the jewellery shops do some monetary business, but to our knowledge they are not entrusted with deposits of savings.

Money loans can, in the first place, be obtained from friends and relatives. This is a common Chinese practice repeatedly described in the literature.[40] Again, loans can be obtained from marketing middlemen with whom the gardener maintains other economic ties. The sums from this source will be limited and the use of these men's lending services does not seem very widespread. This situation resembles that of the fishing village of Kau Sai, where a fish dealer provides advances for a future catch. As a commission he charges his debtors six per cent. There are other dealers who charge only three per cent.[41] This credit institution operates on the basis of personal knowledge. As no Sha Tin informants have used, or admit their use of, marketing middlemen as money-lenders we cannot pursue the comparison. Marjorie Topley informs us of the practice of middlemen to provide credit and their paying in advance for standing crops.[42] We have not heard of this in Sha Tin, but it relates to a common practice in pre-communist China.[43]

One form of credit is that landlords may postpone the time for the payment of rent. Otherwise there is nothing to indicate that they should act as money-lenders for their tenants. This is in contrast to the reporting of Chen Han-seng from Guangdong in the 1930s.[44] The Sha Tin immigrant has very limited contacts with his landlord. Nor is the latter likely to trust the outsider. Money transactions between villagers occur, but to judge from the case we know the details of tenant gardeners could hardly afford to pay the high interests involved, nor can they provide any security.[45] High rates of interest are traditional. In the nineteenth century a businessman in Tai O on Lantau Island in the New Territories made credit agreements with farmers charging a simple interest of 50 per cent of the principal per annum. This is paralleled by the money-lending activities of a *tang* league in the Shek Pik area on the same island.[46]

An interesting finding is that credit opportunities offered from governmental sources are hardly ever used. We believe that this is due to cumbersome and slow procedures which restrain most farmers from all attempts to approach this wealth. We have pointed out that exceptions exist but in a Sha Tin perspective it seems to us as if Marjorie Topley, in her survey article on the New Territories, has painted too bright a picture of governmental success in this field.[47] Furthermore, the Vegetable Farmers' Co-operative Society of Sha Tin does not function well and its membership is limited to 26 persons. This means that a Sha Tin farmer cannot rely on this institution as a contact agency between him and the Department of Agriculture. The Society does not generally negotiate loans on behalf of the local farmers. Nor is there a 'revolving fund', mentioned by Topley as characteristic of most co-operative societies, in operation.[48]

We pointed out that the import of food from the People's Republic of China constitutes half of the supply of the Hong Kong market. The imported produce tends to be low-priced. Variation in the import accounts for variation in the balance between supply and demand on the market, a feature which gives rise to fluctuating prices. Again, we should not entirely neglect the fact that price behaviour of vegetables in urban markets in China has always been unstable.[49]

Owing to high wages and the lack of experienced men, hired labour is rare.[50] We have not heard of anything similar in Sha Tin to the corps of skilled farm labourers who were hired by the peasants in Panyu for the making of garden beds in the fields.[51] Nor have we heard of the existence of hired expert advisers corresponding to the *daqing* - 'Great Green' - as he appeared on Honan Island outside Canton in pre-communist times.[52] The only person who may fulfil a similar function is the local field officer of the Department of Agriculture who is stationed in the office of the Sha Tin Rural Committee. He is expected to tour the area and extend assistance. In those parts of Sha Tin where we have worked not one of our informants knew of his existence.

In Sha Tin it often occurs that some member of the farmer's household is a wage earner in the city areas and commutes between the farmer's cottage and the place of work. The benefit of these external incomes to the farming household seems to vary a great deal owing to the wage earner's position, age, and sex. Jack Potter found in Ping Shan that external incomes were not very important in the rural economy.

In many cases a large part of the earning of these people is not available to meet family expenses. Some of the unmarried sons and daughters do not contribute any of their wages to their parents, and among those who do, the amount contributed varies

> from person to person. A large proportion of the
> income of family heads working in the city is spent
> on food and lodging and in many instances the
> remainder is 'wasted' in gambling halls, tea-houses,
> and dance halls. Thus a great portion of the money
> earned in the city never returns to the village.[53]

It appears to us that individual selling by the
producer directly to the consumer is the kind of
marketing much preferred in Sha Tin. Similar prefer-
ences are hinted at in the literature on pre-communist
China, and Taiwan. In areas where cash crops are not
aimed at metropolitan marketing, peddling of vegetables
is a common feature. So we are told that the lakeside
villagers near Da Hu in Jiangsu Province produce large
quantities of vegetables and find their market among
nearby settlements. There the sellers carry their
produce by boat and visit the surrounding villages.[54]
The peddling may be seen as a different kind of
adaptation in the absence of greater urban centres in
which the marketing could be concentrated. A spreading
out of the 'consumer area' is a prerequisite for
successful gardening enterprises in the 'producer area',
when the local nearby markets cannot avail themselves
of a large and specialized production.

We are not told whether this shipping activity
involved any kind of co-operation between parties concerned but there are reasons to believe that not all
boats set out in the same direction on the same day,
but rather that there may have been some conventional
order in the operations, producing a fanning out of
the departing vegetable barges. Perhaps there were
established zones of interest, but this is only guesswork.

Available information from central Taiwan draws
attention to similar problems.

> Often some of the men in Hsin Hsing who grow the
> same vegetables co-operate in the marketing operation.
> Since the market price is usually about the same in
> each one of the three markets, the men agree in
> advance where each will go to sell his vegetables.
> This prevents any one market from being flooded with
> a vegetable and thus lowering the price.[55]

This, surely, is a minimal form of co-operation in a
traditional situation which implies a reduction of the
forces of competition by way of mutual avoidance.
Again, it is interesting to see how the pedlars in

111

Jiangsu, in the absence of immediate competition and
thereby comparison of prices, operating on their own as
they are, have but very vague ideas about fair prices:

> The pedlars start with only a general expectation of
> a gross return and do not insist on a fixed price for
> each particular transaction. The seller offers a
> price, for instance, two coppers for three sweet
> potatoes. The buyer will not negotiate on the money
> value, but after the money has been given to the
> seller she will take several extra pieces. The
> seller may resist or pretend to resist, but I have
> never seen the transaction repudiated because the
> buyer takes too much. Such a kind of bargaining is
> made possible by various factors: the seller has no
> rigid conception of price, and the buyer has no
> rigid idea of his demand.[56]

The ethnographer, however, concludes that in the long
run, prices determined by this kind of bargaining are
not higher than the market price in the town, as otherwise the urban market would provide a better alternative
for the buyer (or the seller if his gains are lower than
what is offered in the market town). But the information on this issue is rather vague and it is not at
all self-evident that the large margins for fluctuation
in particular transactions, mentioned in the Jiangsu
report, leave the pedlar with a gross return which will
equal over time his possible gains in an urban market;
lack of comparative knowledge implied by the fluctuations
described is not only a situational constraint, but is a
factor which may have more far-reaching effects.
When farmers must sell in one local market, as is the
case in Sha Tin - where Tai Wai is not open, but
restricted to tenants of stalls - they must live with
competition, not only competition between themselves but
with the established retail dealers in the market place.
There are no pedlars in the valley who try to find
customers outside of the market towns. The competition
with regular stalls is even hotter in the metropolitan
area for those who venture to sell their vegetables
there; the hawker in the city may be caused much
trouble by the licensed retailers.[57] In a competitive
situation in the consumer area there is not much to
invite co-operation between different producers living
in a particular neighbourhood. But on the other hand
there seems to be little animosity fostered by the
marketers. Such conflicts as arise do not seem to

originate in the consumer area, but in the producer area
and for reasons not connected with marketing transactions.

We have contrasted the competitive marketing, like
that in Sha Tin, with notes on non-competitive selling
of produce in other parts of China and suggested that a
widespread knowledge of current prices in the former
tends to standardize price expectations, whereas much
uncertainty pertains to isolated transactions when the
actors cannot communicate with others. It might even
be suggested that in a place like Sha Tin Market where
there is intense competition for largely 'fleeting'
customers prices are not set by laws of supply and
demand. Rather, it seems to us as if prices are by and
large conventionalized, negotiated in an intense and
continuous discussion of market prices. Fluctuations
might well be brought about by assertions of negotiated
experience - this time of the year string beans fetch
so much usually and this year will not be very different.
Supply and demand do play important parts. The day
after a typhoon, for instance, prices are considerably
higher for fresh-cut vegetables than under normal
conditions. In an ordinary market morning each seller
of string beans will charge the same price. The
current price is quickly negotiated in the early
mornings in the tea-houses and in street conversations.
Sellers do not compete with price, but with quality.
And in the last resort with luck.

It is interesting to find mention in the literature
that conscious attempts are made in urban markets to
constrain the diffusion of knowledge of current prices
by way of the use of special sign language. From Hong
Kong it is reported that

> A common practice in selling to retailers was known
> as 'silent dealing': bargaining between the *laan*
> (middleman) and the retailer was conducted by use of
> an abacus . . . and the representative of the farmers
> could not see the agreed price as the abacus was
> hidden from his view.[58]

Similarly, signalling systems were designed to limit
the control of price negotiators in many parts of
China. This is a north China example, from the neighbourhood of Peking:

> Prices in the stores, markets, and fairs were not
> always easy to determine as there was no fixed price

for many articles and usually there was no open
bidding in the market. Sales were made between
individuals and prices were often determined by signs
rather than words, with the sign being made under
cover of the buyer's and seller's sleeves. Their
fingers on the other person's arm set one price while
they might talk about an entirely different one.
This, plus the lack of general inter-village communication, often made it difficult for the farmers to
secure top or even fair prices for their produce.
They kept a general check on current prices by
visiting various markets in the neighbourhood and
getting reports from people who had visited the city
and the town markets.[59]

We have found that transportation is an important
part of the marketing operations in Sha Tin. As soon
as produce is to be brought outside the valley, hired
transport is vital. Broker agencies provide their own
lorries. When such services are not employed, farmers
will have to look for other facilities at hand. There
are vans operating especially to meet such rustic
demands, but many do market transports as a sideline
to other activities and forms of business. The latter
is probably a traditional feature common to all of
China.[60] A very interesting note from the New Territories reports that

A few groups of farmers set up marketing associations
among themselves to break the *laan* (middleman) system.
Farmers got together and bought a lorry and baskets
to bring their crops themselves.[61]

We do not know anything about the background for this
kind of co-operation but it seems to have taken place
in pre-VMO days. If initiative came before 1946 when
there were few immigrants in the New Territories, it is
quite possible that such associations were based on
traditional solidarity groupings like lineage and
village. We learn also that they had arranged for a
representative to retail their crops in the city area,
or to sell them to retailers with whom they established
connexions.[62] This is certainly a most interesting
arrangement but our present information is too scanty
to allow any further penetration of the data. We have
no knowledge about similar co-operation in Sha Tin - and
again, in this connexion we have reasons to regret that
we were not able to collect more information on the
flower marketing lorry allegedly 'belonging to a village'.

Obviously such voluntary marketing associations were aimed at the metropolitan markets where control of events, then as now, was very limited for the farmer.

An important aspect of brokerage is that it handles knowledge and information. A middleman screens his expertise of marketing conditions and will not allow any item of his specialized commercial skill to pass on to his clients. For the client, no matter on which side of the activity, the broker is the agency which can diffuse knowledge to him in the specific form of economic returns. A vegetable broker must, minimally, have two sets of knowledge, one of crops and supply, and another which is an integrated picture of consumer and retailer demands, competition, and social networks. His unique and indispensable position comes from his gift of seeing in two directions and combining what he sees into one single 'fit-in'. It is he who controls marketing processes. The best the producer can hope for is some sort of control of the middleman. This can be achieved on a basis of a relatively balanced reciprocity - the broker needs a supply and the farmer a market - a feature which is represented in notions of trust (*xin*) and plans for long term co-operation.

In a country as large and varied as China we may expect nearly all possible forms of brokerage to exist. We cannot discuss these here.[63] Here we should observe that marketing co-operation is an aspect of brokerage in that a body of people, some appointed from a circle of members, some hired, handle the marketing as go-betweens. Marketing co-operative societies in China are not well known and there is little to say on a comparative basis. There is nothing to suggest that co-operative marketing was technically very different from private forms in any part of China.[64]

In her survey of rural economy in the New Territories, Marjorie Topley has drawn attention to a number of interesting features of the marketing processes and we have had occasion already to make use of her data in our previous discussion. Dr. Topley mentions private middlemen who collect the crops of the farmers and take them to the governmental wholesale market in Kowloon and arrange for their sale there under the auspices of official market salesmen. Such middlemen are described as personal friends of the farmers, who often market their own crops at the same time, or vegetable farmers who have performed this kind of service regularly since the establishment of the Vegetable Marketing Organization. They often provide interest-free loans.[65] We have not encountered any persons providing service on these

conditions in Sha Tin. But reminiscent village-based
brokers are mentioned from Ping Shan in another part of
the New Territories.[66]

The City-based urban dealers, sometimes known as
laan in Cantonese,[67] are also focused on. Topley has
some interesting things to say about these brokers in a
historical context:

> Before the establishment of the wholesale market in
> Kowloon vegetable farmers marketed through wholesale
> middlemen, termed *laan* . . . each *laan* had his own
> centre and his own circle of retail clients . . .
> Under the old system, *laan* often made loans to
> farmers . . . *Laan* operated with their own godowns
> (warehouses), lorries - some had fleet of lorries -
> and baskets for transportating vegetables. Sometimes
> regular retailing clients had shares in a *laan* enter-
> prise. Some *laan* had agents or brokers operating in
> collecting stations in market towns.*Laan* and brokers
> were usually townsmen . . . Brokers were more numer-
> ous in the post-war period when there was a shortage
> of *laan* transport, and some of them operate privately
> selling their services to a *laan* . . . the majority
> of *laan* also are said to have been members of the
> *laan* association which fixed the prices to be paid to
> farmers.[68]

Our experience from Sha Tin is that the illegal middleman's business operates very much along the same
traditional lines. We have not encountered any sub-
brokers operating from Sha Tin Market or Tai Wai. The
collecting lorries are directly engaged by the metropolitan enterprise. However, we do not possess detailed
or definite information on the relation between transportation and illegal market. If private dealers co-
operate today this is likely to be under cover. I have
made a few attempts to secure information from illegal
marketers but have failed. Certainly it is a most
delicate matter to get access to more substantial facts
about their dealings.

What has been reported on marketing in this essay
contrasts with other statements made by Dr. Topley. She
maintains that:

> The majority of vegetable farmers, certainly the
> majority of immigrants, belong to these co-operatives.[69]

As we have seen this is not true for Sha Tin. Furthermore, Dr. Topley holds the view that the Vegetable

Marketing Organization has been able to destroy the
system of private entrepreneurship. The broker
activities should have been weakened during the war
period and later there was a general shortage of
transport. The majority of the vegetable dealers had
also lost their godowns and were short of money for
making loans to farmers and to extend other services.
And when VMO was launched it was

> able to extend its monopoly over sales because of
> its control of the transport of vegetables . . .
> It had the lorries, and was, additionally, given
> exclusive right by Ordinance to transport. veget-
> ables or issue permits to private lorries for
> transportation. The police are supposed to stop
> all lorries carrying vegetables to market without
> permit.[70]

In Sha Tin private enterprisers compete very success-
fully with the co-operative society and the official
marketing scheme. The police do not seem to bother
transportation.

Our investigation suggests that the indigenous
villagers still live in a 'rural rice world'. Such
an overstatement may be useful for an understanding
of the process of change. The rice peasants did not
adjust their farming world to the emerging urban world
in their close proximity by way of shifting to market
gardening. Rather, they have maintained their traditional outlook, and from this position they judge
vegetable farming as socially inferior to rice cultivation. This standpoint springs from the semantics
of agnatic kinship ideology, and rice farming.
Instead, their adjustment lies in their abandonment
of the traditional rice cultivation in favour of jobs
in the city, on ships, or overseas. Paradoxically,
the indigenous villagers remained in their traditional
rice world by giving up rice cultivation.

The main sources of change lie in the urban areas,
in Hong Kong and overseas. On the other hand, ideas
from China have not as yet influenced work organization
and economic thinking much in Sha Tin, although they
have so in other parts of the New Territories. New
ideas flowing into the villages will not disrupt traditional notions concerning land, although land use my
have changed in that land is rented to outsiders,
abandoned or converted into building lots. True, the
intensity of traditional life has been much drained in
the postwar period in the absence of an increasing

number of men, and faced with abandonment of traditional
occupations. As a result of urban, Western week-rhythms
some old festivals have become obsolete while others are
celebrated but in a simple way and at much reduced costs.
Although ritual is less explicit today we cannot deny
its continued presence. People come together for the
main festivals. The charter flights organized for Hong
Kong emigrants to Britain for vacation visits back home,
are timed so as to coincide with major feasts.

External incomes earned in Britain and elsewhere are
converted into local village prestige by way of construction of new and bigger houses in the old village.
Of course, all these symptoms do not imply that the
villagers remain unaffected, tradition, and rustic.
On the contrary, they are very much in the midst of a
dramatic (if not traumatic) transition which will
eventually bring about the emergence of a new industrial satellite town, housing a population of at least
half a million people. We merely wish to point out the
direction of this flux and the conservative forces at
play.

The few native villagers who have engaged in horticulture and floriculture did not venture the shift in
land use until they had access to models in the form of
outsider gardeners. Knowledge could be gained from the
observance of these new sources of information, and the
newly acquired knowledge was translated into changing
patterns of land use. We feel that the general lack of
response to city needs for food in the Sha Tin valley is
due to the proximity of the valley to the city, a feature
which involved people directly in city life and provided
new kinds of employment. Urban jobs were more pres-
tigious and more profitable than traditional farming;
and rice farming was more gentlemanlike and reputable
than the laborious but profitable gardening. How often
have village informants expressed their amazement and
disdain at the sight of toiling immigrant gardeners.
The low social prestige of vegetable gardening is pointed
out by Grant in a discussion of the village of Tai Hong
Wai in the New Territories:

> Unfortunately vegetable growing is low in the social
> scale besides being very laborious so that these
> Cantonese farmers on the richest soil in the colony
> do not make the fullest use of their land.[71]

Marjorie Topley has observed that:

In some areas indigenous farmers could increase their
income by switching to vegetable growing. There are
several reasons why few do so at present. One is
that rice needs less labour, and that they are in a
better position than immigrants to send sons to work
abroad where greater income can be earned than in
Hong Kong's urban areas by unskilled workers . . .
Again, many rice farmers feel they lack the skill of
the immigrants in vegetable growing and cannot
compete with them commercially. Further, vegetable
crops are more readily stolen than rice crops . . .
Another reason is that some farmers hold that rice
growing is more honourable than vegetable cultivation. But religious and social activities do not
appear to be as closely connected with rice growing
in the New Territories as in some Eastern countries,
and it is difficult to assess the importance of this
attitude.[72]

We think that Topley's four arguments are useful and
they apply in a wide sense to large areas in the New
Territories. But we have still to consider the variations that occur and aim at finding explanations which
account for variability in form. For instance, Jack
Potter outlines a gradual process of change in the Ping
Shan area, which is very different from our findings
from Sha Tin. He recognizes four different stages.
The first is the traditional system of two-crop rice
agriculture combined with a few catch crops. The
second stage implies a system of two-crop rice cultivation plus a winter crop of vegetables. There follows
a stage of large-scale vegetable growing to be
succeeded, in turn, by a fourth stage which is a system
of intensive vegetable cultivation. This chain of
consecutive transmutations has commercialized an
agrarian system originally oriented towards subsistence.
   During the first stage the vegetables grown were
mainly for family consumption. Then followed experimentation with slow-maturing kinds, and, if proved
successful, extensive vegetable farming then spread
over the fields and was allowed to occupy more time.

After the war the villagers began to experiment with
commercial vegetable growing on a small scale. At
first, the village farmers gradually introduced
vegetable crops into older agricultural patterns.
Instead of growing sweet potatoes on the fields
during the winter months after the second rice crop
had been harvested, they began to plant a catch

crop of winter vegetables. The first experiments
were so successful that the farmers began to increase
the area of land in winter vegetables, bringing into
cultivation paddy land that had formerly been plowed
to lie fallow during the winter months. As the
farmers discovered the sizeable profits that could be
made from vegetables, they switched increasing
amounts of land from rice to vegetables. In fact,
some rice fields that were suitable in soil quality
and water supply were changed over to the year-round
cultivation of vegetables.[73]

Finally, the slow-maturing vegetables were substituted
for fast-growing ones, because of the possibility of a
greater income.[74] The final stage was initiated in the
late 1950s.

At that time immigrants occupied with intense
gardening had been present in Ping Shan for about ten
years, but apparently their presence had had very little
impact on the farming ideas of the villagers. However,
we should note that only 27.8 per cent of the indigenous
villagers of Hang Mei in Ping Shan were farmers, whereas
the rest were found in a wide range of occupations.
Potter explains this low figure against the background
of traditional landlordism.[75] However, it is obvious
that the urban development in the Colony has supplied
many a Hang Mei villager with a new job. Thus it seems
as if the Ping Shan accommodation to the changing human
ecology has taken two main paths.

One path implies that people give up farming and
find new occupations as wage earners. The other implies
a gradual adjustment of the agriculture to the new
developing city markets.

In order to grasp the diffusion of market gardening
in the New Territories we must comprehend how the related
provinces of knowledge are transferred. No doubt the
Department of Agriculture has encouraged diversified
farming, including the planting of winter catch-crops.[76]
We must think also of the enterprising innovators who
see advantages in new conditions which emerge, and who
are of a flexible and experimental disposition. We find
a few examples of such persons in the available literature which may serve as a basis for comparison. Morton
Fried tells us about the introduction of tomatoes in one
area of Anhui:

The tomato entered Ch'u gardening largely through
the observations which were made by a hired garden
worker in the experimental farm of Nanking

University. He convinced a relative of his, a
tenant gardener in Ch'u, that the plant was worthy
of a trial and supplied him with seed. The mere
exposure of the rural workman to varied conditions
expands his knowledge in ways that would not be
possible if he remained within the narrow compass
of his family.[77]

And from the island province of Taiwan, in a village
not far from the city of Taibei, we learn about a
farmer who has taken up vegetable cultivation:

He is not only an industrious farmer, he is also a
modern farmer. He is one of the few men in the
village who reads the farm bulletins and tries new
methods. He speaks with pride of older generations
coming to ask his father's and grandfather's advice,
but he fails to mention that older farmers now come
to him for information on marketing and the new
insecticides.[78]

Obviously such men pass on their knowledge to others.
They are paragons of economic excellence and models
for action among their fellow villagers. Their social
position and prestige will certainly influence their
following with regard to numbers from the standpoint
of receptivity in accepting innovations.

In his description of a village, Nanching, in Punyu
District outside Canton, C.K. Yang draws the following
conclusion, saying that the tropical peasant's

mental outlook was conditioned by the simple or
organic cycle of his crops. His economic ties with
the urban centers and his occasional visits there
did not change the basic conditioning factors
relentlessly exerted upon him by the simple, cyclical,
demanding, and poorly remunerative farm schedule. The
rich and complex urban culture standing at close
proximity to him failed to inculcate in him an urban
way of life. So the peasants of Nanching, only five
miles from a great city and economically related to it,
remained bound to their agrarian tradition; and the
novelties and fascinations of the city appeared to
them totally incongruous to their compelling earthy
scheme of existence, however socially and economically
restrictive such a scheme might be.[79]

Yang's account disagrees with our description of Sha Tin
and the New Territories. Although Nanching people had

responded to city market demands by reorienting part of
their land toward vegetable cultivation, rice farming
was retained as the basic occupation in the village.
We guess that the notion of 'the simple organic cycle
of his crops' refers to rice and that the 'mental
outlook' discussed is based on the set of values and
the meaning invested in rice cultivation.

It is interesting to note that Yang maintains that
a traditional agrarian world view was preserved in
spite of the fact that Nanching had seen a great deal
of emigration implying both long-term and seasonal movement. Yang does not credit this process with any
impact on the local village scene. This is different
from Sha Tin where urban modes of life do penetrate the
rural communities. But, if our reading of Yang is
correct, there is still a fundamental similarity
between the two social situations. An underlying
structure of meaning, traditionally translated into
rice farming and a sequence of ritual events, is
today giving rise to economic activities which are
much more varied, whereas the ritual, although faded
and superficially anachronistic, remains.

An important rule governing the cultural process is
that the unit of rice and land must not be dissolved;
consequently market gardening violates the semantics
underlying land and cultivation. The occupation of
gardening becomes acceptable only when it is carried
out by an outsider who has no bonds with the agnatic
source of land. Thus we think that Eugene Anderson's
statement that competitive market conditions have
become the prime determinants for land use in the New
Territories much too simple. Anderson believes that:

> Under the pressures of the market the rice land
> has been turned to vegetable land, and the old
> village self-sufficiency broken down. Cash-
> cropping monoculture has replaced self-sufficient
> polyculture with direction by the lineages.[80]

In doing so he certainly misses important features of
the social situation of the New Territories.

Still we must account for the villagers who actually
have taken up market gardening. The access to new
knowledge is one variable stressed already. We argue
that these villagers act on the basis of another and
external province of meaning which, although it is in
opposition to tradition, is still part of a new
ontological reality, manifest in the presence of outsider gardeners. The demands to subsist require that

the villager makes a choice between, on the one hand, giving up rice farming for wage earning, in which case he retains the traditional ideology, and on the other, switching to cash crops, and thereby taking on a new set of ideas relating to land. The latter procedure does not necessarily mean that the person loses all contact immediately with his traditional 'rice world'. Potter's data from Ping Shan show how the peasants there for some time tried to span and integrate both provinces of meaning, and that the simultaneous existence of the two sets gave rise to transitional forms. Vegetable crops were introduced into older agricultural patterns. This was only, as Potter rightly points out, a transitional stage, which means that the change was slow and tentative, whereas in Sha Tin, as far as we know, the shift was done swiftly.[81] Perhaps this difference could be related to lower rice yields in the latter area. In Sha Tin it is difficult, not to say hopeless, to survive as a rice farmer, and if it is difficult or less attractive for some reasons to get a job, only vegetable and flower cultivation provide an answer.[82]

One conclusion of this essay is that the immigrant market gardeners live in an 'urban business world'. They are urbanites exploiting the countryside, and they constitute one example of many of an 'overspill' of the city area into the rural landscape. The immigrant farmers have an urban background or are under the leadership of mentors having such experience. The successful gardener is of a merchant background and his prosperity seems related to his ability to run an integrated farm business. In contrast, the less successful gardener's enterprise is an agglomeration of crops with no obvious meaningful interrelationships. Again, the former sophistication emanates from urban shop and trade management, while the latter naïveté springs from unskilled work in town and country. Whatever their previous experience, all are born in rustic villages and have their roots in the rural tradition which accounts for their capability to acquire the manual technical skills and their willingness to leave the bustling life of Chinese cities.

There is little of comparative use in the available literature on China. This does not mean that Sha Tin stands out in uniqueness. Rural urbanites have hitherto remained largely unobserved, but Morton Fried seems to have seen something similar in Anhui:

The farm operators who raise field crops . . .
differ greatly from the town-based cultivators
who specialize in truck gardening. These differ-
ing conditions affect all aspects of the
respective subcultures; family structure, organization of the labour budget, standard of living,
religious life, dependence on the market situation,
are only a few of the areas of difference.[83]

1. Kulp 1925:96.
2. C.K. Yang 1959:31. Belts of cash crops surrounding dense urban areas are of course not confined to China but form a common phenomenon pertaining to city growth.
3. C.K. Yang 1959:76f.
4. Feng & Yung 1931:178.
5. Chen 1936:97.
6. Kulp 1925:84.
7. M. Yang 1945:199.
8. Stenz 1906:846.
9. Fei & Chang 1947:208.
10. For descriptions see Gray 1875:643, 648f, Hardy 1911:26, and Henry 1886:54.
11. Nacken (1873), 1968:133.
12. Hayes 1970:161. See also pp 157, 170, and 174f, and further Hayes 1966:124f. Again, a great deal of vegetable cultivation was to be found on Hong Kong Island soon after the arrival of the British - see Johnston 1846:3 and Hayes 1969:35.
13. Hayes 1970:170.
14. Cf. Aijmer 1967:58f and Aijmer 1976a.
15. Note also the description by Fei & Chang (1947:207ff) from Yunnan which tells us that vegetable cultivation there developed in what appears to be a lineage village with many outsider tenants. However, it is interesting to find that vegetable land was used and controlled entirely by the villagers themselves. This fact contradicts my implicit suggestion that the presence of outsiders may be seen as a crucial condition for this kind of change in land use, and thus limits its validity generally. There were out-siders but they were not, so far as we can judge, agents of change.
16. Potter 1968:35.
17. Potter 1968:36.
18. Potter seems more doubtful on this issue than our quotations reveal, citing Gibbs 1931:132ff to the effect that market gardening in the 1930s was still concentrated mainly in the villages near the city of Kowloon.
19. C.K. Yang 1959:34. Fei & Chang (1947:212) give a detailed account of the corresponding cycle of cultivation in Yunnan.
20. Fried 1953:127.

21. Fried 1953:128.
22. Potter 1968:59.
23. C.K. Yang 1959:34. Cf. also Fei & Chang (1947: 212) whose argument assumes a homogeneous knowledge among the 177 households, of the cultivation of the various kinds of vegetables grown in the village of Yuts'un. They claim that in this Yunnan village the maximization of profits (in combination with personal consumption patterns and soil quality) under- lie the choices in the production made by the farmer.
24. For descriptions of work procedures similar to those of Sha Tin, see Osgood 1975, I:139ff, Potter 1968:67ff, and C.K. Yang 1959:34f.
25. M. Topley 1964:164.
26. Fei & Chang 1947:235.
27. Potter 1968:81.
28. Potter 1968:81f.
29. Chen 1936:54.
30. Potter 1968:69f.
31. M. Topley 1964:172.
32. C.K. Yang 1959:29.
33. Potter 1968:87.
34. M. Topley 1964:177.
35. Ward 1954:198,210.
36. Potter 1968:129.
37. Chen 1936:87f, M. Topley 1964:177, C.K. Yang 1959:70.
38. Potter 1968:159.
39. M. Yang 1945:192.
40. Chen 1936:87, Potter 1968:157.
41. Ward 1954:211.
42. M. Topley 1964:180.
43. Chen 1936:93f.
44. Chen 1936:87.
45. p. 55.
46. Hayes 1967:94 and 1965:119ff.
47. M. Topley 1964:173.
48. M. Topley 1964:195. But the two pig breeders' societies seems to have this function.
49. Cf. Chen 1936:6 and C.K. Yang 1959:29.
50. Cf. Osgood 1975,I:122f, Potter 1968:76f and M. Topley 1964:164f.
51. C.K. Yang 1959:34.
52. Feng & Yung 1931:176.
53. Potter 1968:148.
54. Fei 1939:245. It would be interesting to know how specialized vegetable growing has evolved in the absence of major urban centres.
55. Gallin 1966:63.

56. Fei 1939:245.
57. Cf. M. Topley 1964:180.
58. M. Topley 1964:179f.
59. Gamble 1954:282. For cheating practices in the markets of Sichuan in the 1940s, see Buck 1943:25.
60. See for instance the description by Fei & Chang (1947:190f) of the marketing of home-made paper in Yunnan. On Hong Kong see M. Topley 1964:180. See furthermore Gallin's report (1966:77) from Taiwan where storage is important also.
61. M. Topley 1964:180.
62. M. Topley 1964:180.
63. For some examples illustrating variability see Gamble 1954:280f, Fei & Chang 1947:48, 171, Potter 1968:48f, Fei 1939:254, Fei & Chang 1947:86, 91, Fried 1953:128, Gallin 1966:63f.
64. I have only access to the short notes by Buck (1943:21) on Sichuan. However, other titles exist.
65. M. Topley 1964:179.
66. Potter 1968:48f.
67. *lan* in standard Chinese.
68. M. Topley 1964:179f.
69. M. Topley 1964:173.
70. M. Topley 1964:181.
71. Grant 1960:116, and see also p. 118 for similar statement on the Hakka village of Chuk Hang.
72. M. Topley 1964:170f. See also Pratt 1960:150.
73. Potter 1968:60. In 1950, an official report states more generally that 'very noticeable has been the increased quantity of winter vegetables grown and marketed.' Keen 1950:3.
74. Potter 1968:60f.
75. Potter 1968:44ff, 50.
76. Cf. Grant 1960:118f.
77. Fried 1953:222.
78. Wolf 1968:95.
79. C.K. Yang 1959:35.
80. Anderson 1968:45.
81. In 1953 in the New Territories water chestnuts were planted extensively in place of the second rice crop, but the market was overestimated, and some loss was sustained. This examplifies a widespread attempt to introduce a cash crop into the traditional agricultural pattern. How such waves come about in the New Territories remains a problem. In this particular case the incentive was provided when the United States authorities stated that they were willing to permit imports to some extent. See Teesdale 1954:5, and Cater 1954:28. Cf. also Fei & Chang (1947:212)

who provide an example of how planning for crops is based on the experience from the previous year.

82. M. Topley (1964:171) mentions a lineage in the New Territories which has reinforced its kinship structure by way of switching over to vegetable gardening and the formation of a village-based co-operative society. She does not elucidate further. Perhaps the maintenance of one rice crop, a common practice, a link with the old rice tradition is retained.

83. Fried 1953:23.

X. EPILOGUE: ECONOMIC MAN IN SHA TIN

The study of rational decision-making finds its modern
origin in scholars like Thomas Bayes and Daniel
Bernoulli who in the eighteenth century provided early
formulations about man involving himself in games with
intentions to win. The modern corner-stone is, of
course, the influential work of John von Neuman and
Oskar Morgenstern. I am not sure who introduced the
term 'economic man' into social science to label individuals in the midst of making up their minds as to how
to act best to receive economic advantages. An
economic man maximizes expected value of his wealth,
gain or other utility such as rewards and penalties.
The economic man is a consistent player in a game, who
assigns personal probabilities (which are sometimes
objective) to events, and some sort of numerical
utilities to the thought-of results of his actions, and
advised by this chooses the action of the highest
expected utility. Probably there are more refined ideas
in economics, but unsophisticated sociologists and
anthropologists have worked along these lines. In
anthropology the notion of economic man was first
attacked by Malinowski and other thinkers of a function-
alist leaning, people who gave emphasis to institutions,
exchange, and ritual, rather than to individual economic
management. Still, the notion of man involving himself
in games has thrived in anthropology.

This is not the place for a discussion of 'rational
choice' as an analytic device in anthropology. Con-
troversies there are and we shall not try to solve them
here. Rather we shall take an interest in Sha Tin
economic activities from a slightly different angle
than in previous descriptive and comparative chapters.
In order to have a guideline for our attempts at
formulating this interest we shall employ more explicitly
the notion of economic man, intuitively taken in the
broad sense outlined above. We shall discuss how economic
actors operate in and between such social artifacts as
anthropologists generally refer to as customs and
institutions. In this effort we will adopt an idea that
not all acts are equally explainable on the same level of
analysis; observable economic behaviour springs from
intentions and conventions of a highly diverse nature.

The most shallow analysis we can think of in social
anthropology is one which draws on Skinnerian metaphors.
A basic idea in this widespread positivistic sort of
thinking, and the major conclusion of literally

thousands of studies in sociology and anthropology, is
that most behaviour patterns of interest to the student
arc learned, maintained, extinguished and modified by
means of differential reinforcement and punishment.
This behavioural model of man is explicitly construed in
terms of B.F. Skinner's paradigm of animal studies,
especially of pigeons and mice.

To the anthropologist, the behavioural paradigm is
of limited interest. Few of us, however, will deny
that individual behaviour is well worth studying.
Behaviour in its own right may be of more interest
though for the student of readily observable tokens of
performance in an experimentally determined stimulus-
input and response-output sequence. The anthropologist
who relics on field observations will refer to
observational data on overt behaviour for which it is
impossible to determine either antecedent stimulus
conditions or the internal processing within the
organism. Again, when we as observers look at the
social world, we see behaviour, not structure. An
anthropologist does not generally count units of
behaviour to establish structure although he knows well
that certain things are very repetitive. His knowledge
is intuitive. In common with all other men, the
anthropologist seeks to interprete and draw connections
from his observations; he looks for pattern and meaning
in terms of combinations rather than frequencies.

The anthropologist shares with other sociologists
the ambition to provide propositions about human
behaviour in general which can be applied to a variety
of phenomena, including interactions and social exchange.
He does not necessarily see it as wrong to say that if
something is known to reinforce a particular activity
at a specific time and place, one may assume it is
likely to reinforce other behaviour patterns at other
times and places as well. How we shall know reinforcement is, however, to the anthropologist a highly
problematic question. How can we know when physio-
logical and cultural requirements are not met with,
when a person is 'deprived' and when these requirements
have been met, when a person is 'satiated'?

It is not much help either to realize that deprivation and satiation are matters of degree, that the
states change over time and may vary among individuals
of the same culture. But even if we could handle these
things we would certainly miss out on the more essential parts, that is everything which goes beyond the
learning of stereotyped forms. If we are to develop
beyond this level of shallow analysis which only allows

for the mapping of superficial structures, and move on
to a level of more complex analyses of social structure,
it is necessary for us to comprehend the meanings
attached to conduct by participants. But before we
pursue this, let us see whether there are features of
social and economic life in Sha Tin which with some
advantage could be explored and understood in terms of
the states of deprivation and satiation.

It might be possible to argue, for instance, that
the circumstance that the summer rains on the South
China coast do not fall evenly over the twenty-four
hours, but the largest amounts come in the early morning,
is a reinforcement of the general habit of the vegetable
and flower cultivators to do most of their manual irrigation in the afternoon during the summer season. It is,
so to say, a response to a stimulus, when a gardener
does not water his fields in a rainstorm. If rain
comes in the mornings, and even watering is required,
then we have two conditions and a reasonable response
to them to account for, by way of explanation, a social
pattern of working rhythm. We deem this explanation as
true, but judge it of very limited interest. In fact,
it will immediately give rise to more interesting
questions as to how people show foresight in their
planning of everyday activities and how climatic factors
enter the ongoing process of planning. But raising such
questions we remove ourselves from a position which
seeks explanations in factors of deprivation and
satiation.

A similar case, and this time relating to social
conditions, is to be found in the process of marketing.
We have pointed out that it seems to us as if fear of
disrespect and bad experience of some people in the
valley are features which affect the vegetable producers'
planning for marketing. The drivers and crews of the
lorry fleet of the official Vegetable Marketing Organization often openly show contempt and behave rudely to
their rustic clients. Thus avoidance of the VMO may be
seen as a direct response to the stimulus of rudeness.
But many other factors play more important parts in the
choice between different marketing alternatives. It is
true, of course, that if a gardener goes to the VMO
collection station, he will receive a kind of social
punishment, which, in turn, will have to be balanced with
the possible rewards he may find in selling through this
agent. We are inclined to believe that the avoidance of
contempt is a very strong force in human activities, but
it is mainly a component of emotive import. If a
gardener has two marketing alternatives of just about

equal utility, it is, it seems to us, quite likely that
his disposition to disregard in connection with one
will tip the balance in favour of the alternative.
Rewards in terms of pleasantness and esteem, and punishments in terms of slighting and mockery are active
components in any social and economic decision, but in
themselves they have little explanatory power. To
understand economic acts it is not enough to look for
standardized responses to given factors. We must try
to look into the intentions of the actors.

We have said above that anthropologists who study
non-arranged social situations outside of experimental
laboratories, find it difficult to establish the pre-
conditions of social actions from their observations.
The anthropologist has to make conversations with his
informants to gain accounts of how the actor, while
performing the act, translates his intentions into
behaviour. It may be that the best part of social
activity in any society is stereotyped and displays
advanced uniformity. But we, as anthropologists, are
not particularly interested in how such patterns are
learned under gentle coaxing with rewards and threats
of punishments, nor can we see possibilities of finding
out how stimuli trigger off patterned, reward-punish-
ment learned behaviour. Anthropologists look for how
patterns emerge from planning and negotiation within
the possibilities given by a culture and on a social
scene; cultural competence gives the actor the range
of possibilities and social competence (or kompetence to
follow Rom Harré) guides his intuition about what is
appropriate and correct in any given situation which
unfolds to him. Thus focus is on meaning rather than
substance and in any mode of action he sees a possible
vehicle of meaning.[1]

We have pointed above to some social and economic
features which may be explained by a reference to a
direct response to an input of stimuli. We did point
out also that even a 'direct' response does not entail
an absence of intention. The actor has always an
intellectual attitude to the world. We shall now see
to what extent more complex structures of thought
become important for an understanding of the Sha Tin
scene.

Within the realm of economic life there are
relatively few situations which unfold unexpectedly
and provoke the farmer to immediate interpretation and
hasty action. Few strangers emerge out of nowhere
(anthropologists excluded) and such people are generally
of little economic consequence. Picknickers and hikers

roam the countryside in the week-ends and may destroy
growing crops. A squatter patrol may start inquiries
about a cottage or a shed and have to be bought off.
Fleeting relationships characterize the market towns,
and many of the customers are not known personally by
the vegetable vendors, some are not even recognized.
It is our experience that encounters between sellers
and buyers are short and seldom accompanied by small
talk. Customers inspect in silence and ask for prices
while poking around in the baskets or handling the items
displayed. They are answered shortly. Sellers seem,
on the whole, passive; they seldom solicit clients or
advertise their produce by calls or signs. It is the
customer who has to find the vendor, and the marketer
seems to resort to his good luck.

Intentions cannot be inferred from what people
achieve, but the anthropologist has some opportunity
to study intention as expressed in planning for
activities. No doubt, intentions are constantly re
formulated in processes of planning. In the marketing
situation there is little to contradict the fact that
the gardeners wish to gain as large a return as possible.
In everyday planning for marketing the gardener compares
the expected utility of the various options to reach the
vegetable consumers with regard to his relative abun-
dance in those crops he is about to harvest. It seems
to us that in the marketing situations the Sha Tin
farmer appears as a true economic man. There are
exceptions. We have mentioned that farmers with
specialized crops have, with very little option, tied
themselves to one particular middleman; for them
marketing has become a routinized technique, while
the problem of selling produce has been settled once
and for all.

Part of the marketing game is to find out about
current prices, predict price behaviour, and accommodate
your own crops, if at all possible, to the market demands.
One must also chose the right market with regard to price
and size of crop. The Sha Tin economic man must be a
constant information seeker, and the kind of knowledge
he needs can be obtained from friendly neighbours (not
all neighbours are friendly) who have just returned from
a marketing expedition, or from the general tea-house
conversations during which much of the price negotiating
of the local markets takes place. Thus social knowledge
and access to information over personal networks are
important components in the economic man activities of
the Sha Tin farmers. The social involvement of the
gardeners is something that will be treated elsewhere,

but it should be obvious to the reader that the importance of such circumstances as from whom you get what
kind of information is a very prominent part of the
condition for successful decision making. Confidence in
information received hinges on social relations and is
described as trust.

A farming life requires the development of long term
strategies, the foundation of which concerns the farmer's
relation to his land. Some villagers in Sha Tin do their
long term planning speculatively and reputedly sell their
fields to urban land speculators, deposit the money
gained in a bank which provides an interest on the
deposited capital which surpasses the profits to be
obtained from two crops of rice on the land sold. Other
villagers let their land to outsider immigrants.

The outsider gardeners feel that their rustic alternative is the best possible for them; they know the city
areas and the conditions for urban jobs, and do not want
them. In Sha Tin they earn more, and they are on their
own. We have pointed out that some farmers are but
temporary guests in the countryside, people who try
something different when city jobs are rare. Such
people are prone to come and go, but those who invest
committedly in gardening do so with an intent to remain
in farming for life. In contrast to the villagers they
are landless and have no assets for involving themselves in land speculation (although some passing of
land contracts occur), nor do they generally possess
the manipulative sophistication necessary as their knowledge about the greater Hong Kong scene is often very
vague. They do know, however, that their occupancy of
the land is but a temporary arrangement and that Sha Tin
is planned to become an urban area, a satellite city of
Kowloon. There will be precious little room for
gardeners in that city, and Keng Hau, for instance, will
be covered by massive residential areas. At the time
of our investigation people did not seem to bother too
much about this. Other things were more important at
the time; the political struggle and general unrest of
the late 1960s made many people think that the development plans would never come off.

When a gardener plans for the future, paradoxically
this future does not include his children. People do
not wish their children to remain on the farm or in the
neighbourhood with their own market gardens. If adult
children are around, it is without exception the case
that they cannot find urban employment. Parents try
according to ability to provide the economic means for
some education of their children, most of whom go

through primary school. But secondary schooling in Sha
Tin is much more problematic and costly, and few children
continue their education. Parents hope that their
children will get more 'modern' jobs and the children
and young people we have met all nourish a wish to live
in the glittering city areas.

Some gardens are branches of a domestic economy
centred on wage work. We have seen a couple of examples
of how a family income is diversified by a husband's
earnings in a factory and by the wife's and children's
garden returns. Sometimes the 'external' incomes are
provided by grown-up children. Sometimes such a strategy
of diversification is developed when a man slowly tries
to establish himself as a full-time gardener. At other
times it seems a strategy employed to cushion possible
misfortunes; a double basis provides alternatives in
times of distress caused by upheaval at either end.

In between long-term planning for the future and
immediate calculated response to unfolding situations
there are intermediate plans running according to a
foresight of a stretch of a year ahead in time, or so.
Such plans involve crops to be planted, and although
there may be conventions in this respect to support the
planner, conventions which certainly reflect climate
conditioning and quality of soils; there is also a
certain amount of choice inside the conventional, negotiated framework established. Kinds are chosen to fit
in with temperature and humidity, but often in the hope
that the produce will be early in season to fetch a
higher price. Flowers are planted with an intention to
yield crops at the major Chinese and Western feasts of
the year, especially the lunar New Year.

Such strategic thinking is characterized by short-
comings. One limitation is, as we have seen, the price
behaviour of vegetable produce on the urban market.
The fluctuations are great and when supply is plentiful
owing to imports from China, the prices are sometimes
unexpectedly low. The urban markets are highly unpredictable and it is almost impossible to plan the
vegetable growing as a rational response to forecasts
on fluctuations and demand. In the gardener's planning
there is a strong element of gambling. Another constraint on rational strategy is the difficulty for many
farmers to integrate a multicrop garden enterprise into
one overall system. Each plot has tagged to it its own
plans and expectations, but only few farmers aim at
economic targets with their whole enterprise, as it
were.

The necessity of investments and access to capital
are other constraints on economic choice. If a man
cannot afford to buy the special bamboo trellis and
frames necessary for pumpkins, he does not attempt to
cultivate these. And for some people, their marketing
(and also buying policy) is made with an eye to the
possibility of raising credit in times of need.

We have mentioned already the importance of social
relationships for economic plans and economic knowledge. Besides finding out about prices, for many a
gardener the cultivation of vegetables presupposes the
finding out about techniques. Most of them have their
first venture in gardening here in Sha Tin and in order
to start they have had to learn how to do it from
friendly neighbours and relatives in their vicinity.
Again, the acquisition of pumps was only indirectly
motivated by economic considerations, and these were
triggered by conflicts on the social scene which left
many gardeners with a water problem.

The gardening of vegetables, once you have made up
your mind as to what kinds you opt for, is a process
of conventional planning. The farmer proceeds in a
tunnel of fixed arrangements. How to grow vegetables
is largely conventional knowledge to be drawn from a
corpus of ready-made rules. Judgement and problem-
solving enter the picture only when the application of
techniques raises problems, but seldom is the technique
as such subject to doubts, improvements or analysis.
There are moments of calculation such as when different
fertilizers are used strategically in relation to crops
and time. But by and large, little of individual maximization of utility goes with gardening techniques.

We have seen also in this essay that certain
features of the Sha Tin economic scene cannot be
explained readily by hypotheses of maximization of
expected utility. Issues of morals and meaning become
vitally important for an understanding of the overall
process of agricultural change. The circumstance
that native villagers do not, in general, switch to
vegetable growing from rice cultivation, but rather
adapt themselves to the modern world of Hong Kong by
way of taking up wage jobs, is of utmost importance.
We have argued that the reluctance of the villagers to
make full economic use of their inherited land may be
seen in a semantic context in which the meaning of
rice is a semantic network linking components such as
ancestry - soil - agnatic kinship - domain - belonging -
rice into a powerful emotive and cognitive force which

lingers on beneath the surface of the present day New Territories' realities. Land is to the native an agnatic source.

In Southern China, rice cultivation in flooded fields is, in a traditional context, everywhere endowed with a particular meaning. All activities related to the cultivation of rice are vested with social values. The individual management of the fields by a gardener is not meaningful in the same way for the corporation of agnatic relatives, and is not endowed with prestige, nor can it derive any meaning from lineage ideology. On the contrary, the farms of market-gardening families stand out as anarchistic counterparts to the ideals of the corporate lineage ideology.

Paradoxically, the indigenous villagers have been able to remain in their traditional rice world by giving up rice cultivation. The main sources of change lie in the urban areas, in Hong Kong and overseas. New ideas flowing into the villages will not disrupt traditional notions concerning land, although land use may have changed in that land is rented to outsiders, abandoned or converted into building lots. The few native villagers who have been engaged in horticulture did not venture the shift in land use until they had access to models in the form of outsider gardeners. We feel that the general lack of response to city needs for food in the Sha Tin valley is due partly to the proximity of the valley to the city, a feature which involved people directly in city life. On the other hand we have found that city people have become involved in rural production.

Structures in a society emerge on at least two levels. One type of structure is a phenomenon of accumulation which can be measured, perhaps, by statistical devices. People tend to do similar things in similar situations in a society. Such a mapping of frequencies of behaviour raises questions instead of providing explanations. If people give standardized responses to market forces, for instance, this means that conventions have been nego-tiated, probably for a long time, and they are constantly being renegotiated. We must understand how this is achieved and in this maximization theories will be help-ful. The economic actors can themselves form models of what other people do and such models may become powerful models for what to do. Economic man is, as it were, not only negotiating with other men, but with structures, his own images or models of economic reality.

As we study economic man we will find that important constraints on maximization of utility emerge from

another type of structure. These structures are
semantic in nature and relate to the world through
processes of action and interaction. That people act
according to abstract principles of cultural semantics
is not to be understood, except perhaps in a very
superficial sense, as negotiated conventions. We
cannot explore the theory of culture production here,
but in our Sha Tin context we have argued that
traditional morals and judgements have given agricultural changes a special twist which has fostered
an occupational discrimination between villagers and
outsiders, at the same time turning the valley into a
true suburban area, the villagers engaging in city
jobs, and outsiders bringing a new type of urban enterprise to the old village domain.

The immigrant gardener is an urban enterpriser in
rustic disguise. The outsider-native dichotomy is an
aspect of urban-rural relations at large. We have
shown that this is not to say that urban modes of
life do not find their ways into the villages - there
are many outsider workers living in village houses,
villagers work in Britain or in the city areas, mass
media convey new styles of life. Within a foreseeable
future the whole valley is destined to become a new
satellite city added to the metropolitan complex, a
development now well under way. Everyone knows that
the Sha Tin villages are doomed and soon it will be of
little importance whether you are a native or not.
Meanwhile the villagers suffer the strains of land
speculation, land exchange plans, delayed planning, and
vague official hints. The immigrants who toil on the
land do not pay much attention to these things.
Probably most of them understand that ultimately they
must also go - but to what and where and when are issues
one does not care to think about or let interfere with
what is important now.

NOTE TO CHAPTER X

1. Cf. Aijmer 1976b.

REFERENCES

Agricultural Products Ordinance
    1964   Agricultural Products (Marketing) Ordinance, 1964, *Laws of Hong Kong,* Chapter 277 of the Revised Edition 1964. (Ordinance No. 11 of 1952). Hong Kong: Government Printer.

AIJMER, L. GÖRAN
    1964   *The Dragon Boat Festival on the Hupeh-Hunan Plain, Central China. A Study in the Ceremonialism of the Transplantation of Rice.* The Ethnographical Museum of Sweden. Monograph Series, No. 9. Stockholm: Statens Etnografiska Museum.

    1967   Expansion and Extension in Hakka Society. *Journal of the Hong Kong Branch of the Royal Asiatic Society* 7, 42-79.

    1968   A Structural Approach to Chinese Ancestor Worship. *Bijdragen tot de taal-, land- en volkenkunde* 124, 91-98.

    1972   A Note on Agricultural Change in Hong Kong. *Journal of the Hong Kong Branch of the Royal Asiatic Society* 12, 201-206.

    1973   Migrants into Hong Kong's New Territories: On the Background of Outsider Vegetable Farmers. *Ethnos* 38, 57-70.

    1975   An Enquiry into Chinese Settlement Patterns: The Rural Squatters of Hong Kong. *Man* (N.S.) 10, 559-570.

    1976a   Intercessor Roles in Migration: Recruitment Processes in Rural Hong Kong. *China Quarterly* No. 66, 247-260.

    1976b   A Framework for an Enquiry into Expressive Acts. Part 2: Aspects of Competence. *Working Papers of the Department of Social Anthropology, University of Gothenburg.* No. 2.

    1976c   The Religion of Taiwan Chinese in an Anthropological Perspective. *Working Papers of the Department of Social Anthropology, University of Gothenburg.* No. 9.

    n.d.   Ancestors in the Spring. The *Qingming* Festival in Central China. To appear in *Journal of the Hong Kong Branch of the Royal Asiatic Society.*

ANDERSON, EUGENE N. Jr.
    1968   Changing Patterns of Land Use in Rural Hong Kong. *Pacific Viewpoint* 9, 33-50.

References

BAIRD, DAVID
    1970   Hong Kong: Paradise Gained. *Far Eastern Economic Review* 67, No. 9, February 26:8.

BAKER, HUGH D.R.
    1968   *Sheung Shui. A Chinese Lineage Village.* London: Frank Cass.

BARNETT, K.M.A.
    1955   *Hong Kong. Annual Departmental Report by the District Commissioner, New Territories for the Financial Year 1954-55.* Hong Kong: W.F.C. Jenner, Government Printer.

BARROW, J.
    1951   *Annual Departmental Report by the District Commissioner, New Territories for the Financial Year 1951-1952.* Hong Kong: Noronha & Company, Government Printers & Publishers.

    1952   *Hong Kong. Annual Departmental Report by the District Commissioner, New Territories for the Financial Year 1951-1952.* Hong Kong: Government Printer.

BLACKIE, W.J.
    n.d.   *Report on Agriculture in Hong Kong with Policy Recommendations.* Hong Kong: Government Printer (1955).

BUCK, JOHN LOSSING
    1943   *An Agricultural Survey of Szechwan Province, China. A Summary and Interpretation of a Full Report in Chinese by the Szechwan Rural Economic Survey Committee of the Farmer's Bank of China in Cooperation with the Department of Agricultural Economics, University of Nanking, Directed by Chi-Ming Chiao.* Chunking. Mimeograph.

CATER, J.
    1954   *Hong Kong. Annual Departmental Report by the Registrar of Co-operative Societies and Director of Marketing for the Financial Year 1953-54.* Hong Kong: Government Printer.

CHANG YUET-NGO
    1963   Hong Kong Ts'un (Hong Kong Village) and the Cultivation and Exportation of Incense from Kowloon and the New Territories. In Lo Hsiang lin (ed.). *Hong Kong and its External Communications before 1842. The History of Hong Kong Prior to British Arrival.* Hong Kong: Institute of Chinese Culture.

References

CHEN HAN-SENG
    1936   *Agrarian Problems in Southernmost China.*
            Shanghai: Kelly and Walsh
Cost of Living Survey
    1965   *Cost of Living Survey 1958-63/64. Prepared
            for the Cost of Living Review Committee by
            the Statistics Branch, Commerce and Industry
            Department, Hong Kong, 1st April 1965.* Hong
            Kong: S. Young, Government Printer.
FEI HSIAO-TUNG
    1939   *Peasant Life in China. A Field Study of
            Country Life in the Yangtze Valley.* London:
            Routledge & Kegan Paul.
FEI HSIAO-TUNG and CHANG CHIH-I
    1947   *Earthbound China. A Study of the Rural
            Economy in Yunnan.* Chicago University Press.
FENG RUI and YUNG PING-HANG
    1931   A General Descriptive Survey of the Honan
            Island Village Community. *Lingnam Science
            Journal* 10:153-186.
FIRTH, RAYMOND
    1966   *Malay Fishermen. Their Peasant Economy.*
            2nd ed. London: Routledge & Kegan Paul.
FRANKE, O.
    1913   *Keng Tschi T'u. Ackerbau und Seidengewinnung
            in China, ein keiserliches Lehr- und Mahnbuch,
            Aus dem Chinesischen übersetzt und mit
            Erklärungen versehen.* Abhandlungen des
            Hamburgischen Kolonialinstituts, Bd. 11.
            Hamburg.
FREEDMAN, MAURICE
    1958   *Lineage Organization in Southeastern China.*
            London School of Economics Monographs on
            Social Anthropology, No. 18, London: Athlone
            Press.

    1963   *A Report on Social Research in the New
            Territories.* London School of Economics and
            Political Science. Mimeograph. (Reprinted in
            *Journal of the Hong Kong Branch of the Royal
            Asiatic Society*).

    1966a *Chinese Lineage and Society: Kwangtung and
            Fukien.* London School of Economics Monographs
            on Social Anthropology. No. 33. London:
            Athlone Press.

    1966b Shifts of Power in the Hong Kong New Terri-
            tories. *Journal of Asian and African Studies*
            1:3-12.

References

FRIED, MORTON
    1953   *Fabric of Chinese Society. A Study of Social
            Life in a Chinese County Seat.* New York:
            Praeger.
GALLIN, BERNARD
    1966   *Hsin Hsing, Taiwan: A Chinese Village in Change.*
            Berkeley and Los Angeles: University of
            California Press.
GAMBLE, SIDNEY D.
    1954   *Ting Hsien. A North China Rural Community.*
            New York: Institute of Pacific Relations.
GIBBS, L.
    1931   Agriculture in the New Territories. *The Hong
            Kong Naturalist.* 2, 132-4.
GILES, RAY and YUNG WAI CHUNG
    1966   *A Social Survey of Five Rural Chinese Villages
            and Squatter Areas in the Sha Tin Valley Area,
            New Territories, Hong Kong.* Church World
            Service, Hong Kong, Program Department, Social
            Work Research Unit. Parts I and II. Mimeograph.
GRANT, CHARLES J.
    n.d.   *The Soils and Agriculture of Hong Kong.* Hong
            Kong: Government Printer. (1962?)
GRAY, J.H.
    1875   *Walks in the City of Canton. With an Itinerary.*
            Victoria: n.p.
GROVES, ROBERT G.
    1965a   The Origins of Two Market Towns in the New
            Territories. In *Aspects of Social Organization in
            the New Territories.* Hong Kong: Royal Asiatic
            Society, Hong Kong Branch. n.d.
    1965b   *Report of Field Work in Hong Kong.* London-
            Cornell Project. Mimeograph.
GROVES, ROBERT G. and KENNETH R. WALKER
    1967   Rice Farming in Hong Kong. *The Geographical
            Magazine* 39: 751-763.
HAYES, JAMES W.
    1962   The Pattern of Life in the New Territories in
            1898. *Journal of the Hong Kong Branch of the
            Royal Asiatic Society* 2:75-102.
    1965   Village Credit at Shek Pik, 1879-1895. *Journal
            of the Hong Kong Branch of the Royal Asiatic
            Society* 5:119-122.
    1966   Old British Kowloon. *Journal of the Hong Kong
            Branch of the Royal Asiatic Society* 6:120-137.
    1969   A Chinese Village on Hong Kong Island Fifty
            Years Ago - Tai Tam Tuk, Village under the
            Water. In I.C. Jarvie & J. Agassi (eds.), *Hong
            Kong: A Society in Transition, Contributions*

to the Study of Hong Kong Society. London: Routledge and Kegan Paul.

1970　Old Ways of Life in Kowloon: The Cheung Sha Wan Villages. *Journal of Oriental Studies* 8: 154-188.

HENRY, B.C.

1886　*Ling-Nam, Or Interior Views of Southern China. Including Explorations in the Hitherto Untraversed Island of Hainan.* London: S.W. Partridge & Co.

JOHNSTON, A.R.

1846　Note on the Island of Hong Kong. In: *The Hongkong Almanach and Directory for 1846.* Hongkong: China Mail.

KEEN, K.

1950　*Hong Kong. Annual Report by the District Commissioner, New Territories for the Year Ended the 31st March, 1950.* Hong Kong: Noronha & Co., Government Printers and Publishers.

KING, FRANKLIN H.

1926　*Farmers of Forty Centuries. Or Permanent Agriculture in China, Korea and Japan.* London: Jonathan Cape.

KULP, DANIEL H.

1925　*Country Life in South China. The Sociology of Familism. Volume I. Phenix Village, Kwangtung, China.* New York: Teachers' College, Columbia University.

LAI CHUEN YAN

1964　Rice Cultivation, Distribution and Production in Hong Kong. In S.G. Davis (ed.), *Land Use Problems in Hong Kong.* Hong Kong: Hong University Press.

LLOYD, J.D.

1921　Report on the Census of the Colony for 1921. *Papers Laid before the Legislative Council of Hongkong 1921.* Hongkong: Government Printer.

LO, C.P.

1968　Changing Population Distribution in the Hong Kong New Territories. *Annals of the Association of American Geographers* 58: 273-284.

NACKEN, J.

(1873)　Chinese Street-cries in Hongkong. *Journal of the Hong Kong Branch of the Royal Asiatic Society* 8:128-134, 1968. (Reprinted from *China Review* 2:51-55, 1873.)

References

OSGOOD, CORNELIUS
    1975   *The Chinese. A Study of a Hong Kong Community.*
               (3 vols.) Tucson: The University of Arizona
               Press.
POTTER, JACK M.
    1968   *Capitalism and the Chinese Peasant. Social
               and Economic Change in a Hong Kong Village.*
               Berkeley and Los Angeles: University of
               California Press.
    1969   The Structure of Rural Chinese Society in New
               Territories. In I.C. Jarvie & J. Agassi (eds.)
               *Hong Kong: A Society in Transition, Contri-
               butions to the Study of Hong Kong Society.*
               London: Routledge and Kegan Paul.
PRATT, JEAN A.
    1960   Emigration and Unilineal Descent Groups: A
               Study of Marriage in a Hakka Village in the
               New Territories. Hong Kong. *The Eastern
               Anthropologist* 13:147-158.
Sha Tin Outline Zoning Plan
    (1967) Hong Kong Government, Town Planning Board,
               Plan No. LST/47. n.d.
SMITH, ARTHUR H.
    1899   *Village Life in China. A Study in Sociology.*
               New York: Revell.
South China Morning Post.
         (Hong Kong daily newspaper)
STENZ, G.M.
    1906   Der Bauer in Schantung. *Anthropos* 1:435-452,
               838-863.
TAX, SOL
    1953   *Penny Capitalism. A Guatemalan Indian
               Economy.* Washington: Smithsonian Institution,
               Institute of Social Anthropology.
TEESDALE, E.B.
    1954   *Hong Kong, Annual Departmental Report by the
               District Commissioner, New Territories for
               the Financial Year 1953-54.* Hong Kong:
               Government Printer.
TOPLEY, K.W.J.
    1962   *Hong Kong. Annual Departmental Report by the
               Commissioner for Co-operative Development and
               Fisheries for the Financial Year 1961-62.*
               Hong Kong: S. Young, Government Printer.
TOPLEY, MARJORIE
    1964   Capital, Saving and Credit among Indigenous
               Rice Farmers and Immigrant Vegetable Farmers
               in Hong Kong's New Territories. In Raymond
               Firth and B.S. Yamey (eds.), *Capital, Saving*

144

and Credit in Peasant Societies. Studies from Asia, The Caribbean, and Middle America. London: George Allen and Unwin.

WAGNER, WILHELM
1926 *Die Chinesische Landwirtschaft.* Berlin: Parey.

Wah Kiu Yat Po
(Hong Kong daily newspaper).

WARD, BARBARA
1954 A Hong Kong Fishing Village. *Journal of Oriental Studies* 1:195-214.

WOLF, MARJORIE
1968 *The House of Lim. A Study of a Chinese Farm Family.* New York: Appleton-Century-Croft.

WONG, C.T. & R.S. BRERETON
n.d. *Does it Pay to Grow Vegetables?* Department of Agriculture, Hong Kong Government, mimeograph.

WONG, C.T. & R.R. MASON
n.d. *Factors Affecting Production Planning on Vegetable Farms in Hong Kong.* Department of Agriculture, Hong Kong Government. Mimeograph.

WU HWA-PAO
1936 Agricultural Economy of Yung-Loh Tien in Shansi Province. *Nankai Social and Economic Quarterly* 9:164-176.

YANG, C.K.
(1959) *A Chinese Village in Early Communist Transition,* Cambridge, Mass.: The MIT Press, 1969.

YANG, MARTIN C.
(1945) *A Chinese Village, Taitou, Shantung Province.* London: Routledge and Kegan Paul. 1948.

For Product Safety Concerns and Information please contact our EU
representative GPSR@taylorandfrancis.com Taylor & Francis Verlag GmbH,
Kaufingerstraße 24, 80331 München, Germany

Printed and bound by CPI Group (UK) Ltd, Croydon, CR0 4YY
08/05/2025
01864362-0011